Weekly Insights for the Workplace: ***A Devotional for Christian Professionals***

Agnes Amos-Coleman,
Carolyn Cogswell

WESTBOW PRESS®
A DIVISION OF THOMAS NELSON & ZONDERVAN

WestBow Press books may be ordered through booksellers or by contacting:

WestBow Press
A Division of Thomas Nelson & Zondervan
1663 Liberty Drive
Bloomington, IN 47403
www.westbowpress.com
1 (866) 928-1240

ISBN: 978-1-5127-3336-5 (sc)
ISBN: 978-1-5127-3337-2 (hc)
ISBN: 978-1-5127-3335-8 (e)

Library of Congress Control Number: 2016903595

Print information available on the last page.

WestBow Press rev. date: 03/03/2016

Especially for...

52 Weeks of devotions for the employed, unemployed, business owners, those in transition, and those seeking a spiritual pathway in their career journeys and desiring to use their talents to glorify God.

Discover in this book:

- How to Find God's Will in Your Career
- Spiritual Tips and Prayers for Your Career Journey

Authors

- Agnes Amos-Coleman
- Dr. Carolyn Cogswell

Dedication

We dedicate this book to the glory of God. Without Him, the idea and the collaboration would not have taken place. We declare all honor, adoration, and praise to the Most High God, and we are humbled by the wisdom, knowledge, and understanding that He has bestowed upon us.

Each of us has gone through different career struggles that have manifested themselves in unfulfilled dreams and expectations. However, we held on to Hope and trusted God that we are where we are for a reason, and through this journey we have learned to rejoice and praise God no matter what.

Through the writing of this book, it is our pleasure to tell you about the miraculous signs and wonders that the Most High God has performed for us, and we declare the words of King Nebuchadnezzar in Daniel 4:3 (NIV), because that is the God we serve:

> How great are his signs,
> how mighty his wonders!
> His kingdom is an eternal kingdom;
> his dominion endures from generation to generation.

Acknowledgments

To all our family members—maternally and spiritually. Without their support and inspirations we would not have been able to focus on this project. We are truly blessed to be part of such an amazing family.

The journey of our lives has been shaped by so many people. To all of you (and you know who you are), we say *thank you for not giving up on us* and for your relentless prayers and encouragement.

Endorsement Reviews

Praise the Lord for this good and faithful work by Dr. Carolyn Cogswell and Agnes Amos-Coleman, MBA. This book is chock full of biblical reassurance that throughout the many seasons of our careers we are never alone! Having survived my own share of organizational conflict and office politics, as well as a devastating job layoff, I know firsthand that the Lord is good to those who wait for Him (Lamentations 3:25). You will be blessed as you follow the 52-week journey the authors have masterfully laid before you.

Despite their impressive experiences and testimonies, the authors have not made this book about themselves. Rather, they did a fabulous job of integrating Old and New Testament scriptures, reflections, and affirmations to remind us that the Lord is loving and faithful. They remind us that He has plans for us (Jeremiah 29:11), watches over every detail of our work lives (Psalm 121:8), and will never, ever leave us or forsake us (Deuteronomy 31:6)!

Regardless of your current situation, this devotional will keep you focused on the Lord. He, in turn, will help you fight whatever career battle you may be facing (1 Timothy 1:18). Whether you are employed, under-employed, or unemployed, this devotional will enable you to seek His face, trust His provision, and work each day as if working for the Lord (Colossians 3:23). May He richly bless you!

Don Levonius

Principal of Victory Performance Consulting LLC, USA

The first thing that caught my attention was to keep God our focus while in our work. When I do this I am a better worker. The choices I make reflect the constant realization that He is there. As a result I tend to make better decisions, because I want to please Him. When we view Jesus as our employer, and seek to please Him instead of our boss or peers, there is a peace that follows.

Usually, pleasing God reflects well with work, because we reflect His character. We are not selfishly motivated, knowing our reward is in His hands. But I find peace and joy are a great compensation. That's what we get when we honor Him in our work. Not only this but having the privilege, when appropriate, to share Christ, is very rewarding.

I am a byproduct of a person sharing his faith in the workplace. It didn't get in the way of our work, but it remained constant over the course of a few years. I didn't realize it then, but I was watching this co-worker, wondering why a smart guy like him had gone religious. His faith shining in his work drew me to Christ.

I liked in your devotional reading, the focus you gave. Even to remember to praise God. Having His praise in our heart continually motivates me to live a thankful life. I don't deserve anything, but He has given so much.

A majority of our waking time is spent in working. If we never make time for Christ there, what a waste of life! Especially because He wants to send his blessings.

Your writings, if taken to heart, will help motivate people to rise up and invite God's presence in to their work. Who knows? There may be people like me who are watching and wanting something better in life then this world brings.

Danny Servos

Retired Airline Employee, Canada

This book is an excellent resource for today's faith believers. The daily Scriptural referenced devotions direct the reader to God's

Word as the ultimate source for life instructions and strength. It is a helpful tool for all Christians; especially the one's working in the corporate world, and encourages them to start their day by seeking the Lord. People of faith will be reminded of the importance of being the light God has called them to be—regardless of their work environment or situation. This devotional would be a great addition for any believer.

Pastor Christopher Polke
President and CEO, Chris Polke Ministries, Inc., USA

Many Christians underestimate the importance of inviting and working with the Holy Spirit in their day-to-day activities, either at work, prospecting for jobs, or making a career decision that can change their whole lives. This devotional is a compulsory pathway and guide that will help you walk and work daily with God to bring to manifestation the promises of God for your life. Psalm 119:105 clearly indicates the need for us to be fed daily with the Word of God.

The "Let Us Reason Together" section makes it interactive and different from conventional devotionals. I pray God Almighty will increase His presence in you and your household as you study it daily in Jesus' name, amen.

Christopher Olusola Head
Domestic Banking, Ecobank, Zambia

Our Christian faith can't be left for Sunday use only, yet the pressure in many working environments does not permit thoughts of much other than the immediate tasks being faced. So I welcome this Devotional, which focuses on the Christian in the workplace. A good starting point would be to read each week's Devotional on Monday at breakfast, on the journey to work, or during morning coffee time, and so set one's thoughts on an aspect of Christian living and work for the week ahead.

It isn't always wise or possible to try to discuss one's faith with colleagues while at work, but I still recall the witness of a Christian who worked in the same factory as me many years ago. His work brought him into contact with people of all levels and responsibilities. Everyone spoke well of him. His clear Christian witness was in the way he did his job. As you read this Devotional each week I pray that you may, "Let your light so shine before men, that they may see your good works, and glorify your Father in heaven" (Matthew 5:16, NJKV).

John Wedlake, (Retired), Board Member
Christian in Communication, England, United Kingdom

From time to time we all need encouragement. At any work place as a professional Christian, the challenge is how to respond daily to difficult situation with communication and collaboration toward our colleagues, regardless of their backgrounds. These situations can challenge our faith. We need a roadmap backed up in the Word of God, with selected practical scriptures to provide the encouragement we need in these challenging times. If you are a Christian and a professional in any field, this book is a *MUST READ* book.

Eliane Ramos
Amaral, Brazil

The relevance of this book in the lives of Christians in the workplace is *priceless*. We live in a time when as we look around us we see nothing but hopelessness. Yet Christians in the work place are to be light that cannot be hidden. This book provides inspiration and encouragement on how to live out our Christian faith in the work place.

Linda McNicholl
New Zealand

Contents

Section Three
Dealing With Difficult Situations

Section Four
Struggling for Promotion

Section Five
The Christian's Business Relationships

Section Six
The Provisions of God

Section Seven
Being Light in a Dark World

About this Devotional

You are holding in your hands a 52-week devotional for employed, underemployed or unemployed persons, business owners, those in transition, and those seeking a spiritual pathway in their career journeys and desire to use their talents to glorify God.

As professionals, many times we tend to break our lives up into weeks, rather than days. Because of this, having one devotion a week for meditation tends to simplify our lives as we consider each work week ahead of us.

Based on weekly affirmations that build boldness and confidence, these devotions draw on the Word of God for edification and comfort and for strength for the soul.

In addition to the devotions, the volume contains a section on how to find God's will in your career, along with seven spiritual tips and prayers for your career journey.

Readers will also have an opportunity to make a commitment to serve God, along with spiritual considerations and views to keep focused as they journey through their careers.

As Christian professionals, we view the work world differently than we did before we put our trust in Christ. Whereas we may have looked at our career path as simply a way to put food on the table and pay the bills while we pursue our *real* interests, we now see it as a calling from the Lord. So, let us walk together as we "let your light shine before others, that they may see your good works and glorify your Father in heaven" (Matthew 5:16).

How to Use This Book

> Keep this Book of the Law always on your lips; meditate on it day and night, so that you may be careful to do everything written in it. Then you will be prosperous and successful.
>
> Joshua 1:8

This *Week By Week Devotional* is not a how-to book for the week. The only how-to book we recommend is the Holy Scriptures, because in them we will find that it is through the knowledge of God that we have been given, "everything we need for a godly life through our knowledge of him who called us by his own glory and goodness" (2 Peter 1:3).

Our hope is that through the use of these weekly affirmations and the study of the Scriptures the Lord, by his Holy Spirit, will transform you by the renewing of your mind(Romans 12:2), so that you will grow more and more in harmony with God's perfect will for your life. He has given us these devotions to "consider how we may spur one another on toward love and good deeds" (Hebrews 10:24).

We believe that the more time you spend with the Lord, abiding in Him, talking to Him, and inquiring of Him in His Word, the more you will develop intimacy with the Lord, and the more He will prepare you for those works He has established for you.

> For we are God's handiwork, created in Christ Jesus to do good works, which God prepared in advance for us to do.
>
> —Ephesians 2:10

You will notice that the devotions in this book are different lengths, with different numbers of Scripture references. Some have seven principles, which naturally lend themselves to using one a day throughout the week. Others have six or fewer than six. Some have complete chapters. In these cases, our suggestion is that you pray and ask the Lord to guide you as to how to utilize them. Here are a few suggestions.

1. Write a verse out on an index card and carry it with you all day. Meditate on it when you have a chance throughout the day. You may be able to grab a glance at it before you arrive at work or to a job interview, and ask the Lord to show you how to apply it in your life today.
2. Memorize the verses that particularly speak to you. This will help the Word become more powerful in your life. If you journal, use them in your journaling.
3. Utilize the blank spaces in the book to jot down your thoughts and feelings about the ideas presented in each devotion. We believe the Lord will give you other ideas as you seek Him in all manners pertaining to your professional life.

The First Day of a New Year

Today is the first day of a new year! And if this is the day the Lord has made Psalm 118:24) it follows that, "This is the year the Lord has made," and, "This is the week the Lord has made," and we will rejoice and be glad in it! Isaiah 43:19 says:

> See, I am doing a new thing!
>   Now it springs up; do you not perceive it?
> I am making a way in the wilderness
>   and streams in the wasteland."

This is the first week of a new year. What an exhilarating thought! The possibilities, the blessings, the joy, the comfort of being in the Lord's sovereign care as He makes a way in in the wilderness and streams in the wasteland! Every day I'm going to confess that this is the day that the Lord has made. I will rejoice and be glad in it. God, You are always doing a new thing because You are not only Creator of the world, but You are my Creator, and I am Your workmanship, created in Christ Jesus to do good works which You prepared in advance for us to do! (Ephesians 2:10).

This explains this drive deep within me to seek greatness! God, You have put that within me! You have said in Hebrews 11:6 that, "Without faith it is impossible to please God." I want to please You, Lord. With all my heart when I meet You on the day You return or on the day I pass away from this world, I want to hear You say, "Well done, good and faithful servant" (Matthew 25:21).

Psalm 118:24 Isaiah 43:19 Ephesians 2:10
Hebrews 11:6 Matthew 25:21

Let Us Reason Together

Should we as Christians seek greatness? Sometimes we tend to think of greatness in terms of fame and fortune, but what is greatness in the eyes of God? Certainly, if our goal is to give the entire honor and glory to Jesus Christ (and God knows our heart), it is not unrealistic or wrong for us to be ambitious or to seek greatness in any area of our lives.

Matthew 6:33 (NKJV) says to, "...seek first the kingdom of God and his righteousness and all these things shall be added." "All these things" include food and clothing and everything we need for this life. Since our purpose in life is to know Him and to make Him known, as long as we are pursuing Him, He will provide what we need, and, as David said, He will make us great in His sight. In light of all this, what is your definition of greatness?

Psalm 18:35 Matthew 6:33

As you confess the following affirmation, you will experience your heart's desire.

Affirmation

My life will yield increase!

SECTION ONE

Job Searching

WEEK 2

Count on God's Guidance

Consider such a time when you were led to reach out to a current or old acquaintance, rewrite your resume or cover letters in certain ways, or do things concerning your career that you would normally not have done.

I call this drive divine wisdom, knowledge and understanding from the Lord, and this promise is for those who have dedicated their career path and journey to the Lord. This promise is not to be taken lightly, but instead give God the praise for endowing you with this blessing.

I recall a time in my personal career path when the Lord would guide my heart to call certain people, or tailor my cover letter to position myself for a particular job, and this situation was accepted favorably. On reflection, I am convinced that only Christ in me could have guided me, because I was not smart enough to come up with such ideas.

For the reader of this devotion, He is ever present in your situation as well, and He supernaturally guides your steps. To the world, this is called *coincidence.*

Psalm 37:23 (NKJV) confirms this is ordained by Jehovah: "The steps of a good man are ordered by the LORD, and He delights in his way."

What a great reassurance for you to know that our Lord Jesus Christ is with you all the way—in deciding what jobs to apply for and the contacts to reach out to or the next career move.

Proverbs 2:6 James 1:5 1 Kings 3:12

Let Us Reason Together

The Bible tells us how God can supernaturally choose to fill us with whatever we need to get the job done. Reflect on Exodus 35:30–31: "See, the LORD has chosen Bezalel son of Uri, the son of Hur, of the tribe of Judah, and he has filled him with the Spirit of God, with wisdom, with understanding, with knowledge and with all kinds of skills"

Begin to declare the following affirmation into your life, and you too will be chosen to do mighty works.

Affirmation

Divine wisdom, knowledge, and understanding are mine!

Trust God for a Positive Outcome

Thank you, most high God, for another new beginning. Remember that, "This is the day the Lord has made; we will rejoice and be glad in it" (Psalm 118:24, NKJV). Each day is a gift from God, but there are many who do not see it that way. May I always be grateful for a new day and a new beginning.

Zechariah 4:6 says,

> This is the word of the LORD to Zerubbabel: "Not by might nor by power, but by my Spirit," says the Lord Almighty."

Thank You for the power of Your Spirit working on my behalf. Thank You for the gift of life for me and my household. Thank You that the joy of the Lord will be my strength (Nehemiah 8:10). Thank You that surely goodness and mercy will follow me all the days of my life, and I will dwell in the house of the Lord forever (Psalm 23:6).

Father, thank You that my job searches will come to a glorious outcome this year, in Jesus' name. I choose to start each new day with a positive outlook and trust in the faithfulness of God.

Psalm 118:24 Zechariah 4:6 Nehemiah 8:10 Psalm 23:6

Let Us Reason Together

In both good times and challenging times, do you cultivate an attitude of praise and worship? If not, how could you live today in active awareness of the need to praise God no matter what?

Affirmation

I am singled out for elevation!

Take Each Step With God

It is encouraging to know that You are with us every step of the way, Lord, when we seem to be stuck and don't know for sure which way to go, as well as during those times when things seem to be falling into place. In this way You teach us not to depend on circumstances (or on our own understanding), but on You alone (Proverbs 3:5–6).

You said in John 16:24, "Until now you have not asked for anything in my name. Ask and you will receive, and your joy will be complete." Father, I am asking, and when You give (in Your time), it will be glorious. You are a good and kind God.

In my own job-seeking journey (Agnes), I remember a time when a phone interview I was waiting for went particularly well, and I felt the job I interviewed for was a great fit for me. The employer said they would get back to me if they wanted to pursue my candidacy further.

Although I did not ultimately land that job, the experience prepared me for future interviews, and brought me one step closer to the position God had planned for me in the future. I made sure to send them a thank-you letter and a written sample of my work.

This experience caused passion to rise up within me and made up for past failures. At this point, the next step was a face-to-face interview, so I began to believe God for that. Sometimes God will provide a positive experience such as this one just to energize us and encourage us to give the job-hunting process all we have so that God may be glorified.

I am thankful for every step in the process of developing my potential for Your glory, Lord. Help me to trust in You and not in my own understanding.

Proverbs 3:5–6 John 16:24

Let Us Reason Together

As a child of God, you will pass through crises, not live in them. Think about the children of Israel in the book of Exodus. After four hundred years in their place of crisis, they finally ended up in the Promised Land. As you confess the following, you too shall speedily depart from your crisis situation and move toward your own promised land!

Affirmation

I am coming out of my place of crisis!

WEEK 5

He Is Directing Your Steps

I will extol the LORD at all times;
his praise will always be on my lips.
I will glory in the LORD;
let the afflicted hear and rejoice.
Glorify the LORD with me;
let us exalt his name together.

Psalm 34:1–3

This is my song of thanksgiving to You, Most High God, for Your daily provision. You are so faithful. You hear me when I pray; You answer when I call. You are with me always, and You will keep me in perfect peace when I keep my mind on You (Isaiah 26:3).

When I come to the realization that everything that God allows in my life is for the purpose of growing me up in Him and developing faith, it becomes less of a burden to endure trials, delays, disappointments, and inconveniences. He makes it possible to, "count it all joy when you fall into various trials, knowing that the testing of your faith produces patience. But let patience have its perfect work, that you may be perfect and complete, lacking nothing" (James 1:2-4, NKJV).

Every aspect of the job search can be stressful and difficult and a source of great trials. But just remember, the joy of the Lord is your strength (Nehemiah 8:10). But no matter where you are in the process you know the Lord is directing your steps. This is a great comfort!

Psalm 34:1–3 Isaiah 26:3 Nehemiah 8:10
James 1:2–4

Let Us Reason Together

It is God's will for you to be happy and have peace. In Romans 14:17, the Bible describes the kingdom of God as, "righteousness, peace and joy in the Holy Spirit." If you are not experiencing these God-given gifts, declare the following into your life, and so shall it be.

Affirmation

I am extremely happy and have peace!

WEEK 6

Career Change Miracles

A *miracle* is defined as "an event contrary to the laws of nature and attributed to a supernatural cause." The Bible is full of miraculous events to encourage the people of God. One that stands out in my mind is found in Joshua 10:12–14. In this story, the Lord caused the sun to stand still in the middle of the sky and delayed its going down for a full day.

The Bible offers many reasons why God would go the extra mile to perform miracles. Three reasons could be:

1. He wants us to believe in His sovereignty.
2. He does it out of love and compassion for us.
3. To build our faith in Him

One of the times in our lives to attract God's miracles is when we are faced with career situations—looking for a new job, needing a promotion in the current job, needing our business to prosper, or needing to make a career change. In all these situations, we need God to visit us with a divine miracle.

In my personal life, God has shown up miraculously and blessed me with job offers that I never thought possible. The same God can do likewise for you in your career situation because He is the great I Am and a very present help in time of trouble.

Psalm 46:1 1 Kings 17:13–15 Matthew 9:6–7
Matthew 9:22

Let Us Reason Together

This week, I encourage you to ponder on the area of your life where you want God to intervene with His miraculous power, and begin to declare into your life the following.

Affirmation

My life will attract God's miracles!

WEEK 7

Provision in Transition

The Lord has promised to provide everything we need. *Provider* is even one of His names. So if being our provider is something He is, not just something He does, we should be able rest in that. I remember singing, "Jehovah-Jireh, my provider, His grace is sufficient for me" in the early days of my Christian walk. It was so easy at first. Since then tests have come.

Uncertainty is a given in the midst of transitions in our work lives. Will we get the interview? Will we get the job? Will it be a good fit? How will God provide when I have no income? Will there be enough for the bills? What about giving? Well, what does the Word say about that?

> Give, and it will be given to you. A good measure, pressed down, shaken together and running over, will be poured into your lap. For with the measure you use, it will be measured to you.
>
> —Luke 6:38

> "Bring the whole tithe into the storehouse, that there may be food in my house. Test me in this,"

> says the LORD Almighty, "and see if I will not throw open the floodgates of heaven and pour out so much blessing that there will not be room enough to store it."
>
> —Malachi 3:10

"I was young and now I am old, yet I have never seen the righteous forsaken or their children begging bread," David wrote in Psalms 37:25. God is faithful and his Word is true.

Luke 6:38 Malachi 3:10 Psalms 37:25

Let Us Reason Together

When God calls you to give money, time, talent, or anything else in your time of need (when it hurts the most), do you respond in obedience or disobedience? What are you willing to change in order to obtain different results? Scripture is full of encouragement concerning God's faithfulness and provision for His children in time of need. Reflect on Genesis 22:8, where God asked Abraham to sacrifice his son Isaac. On their journey to the place of sacrifice, Isaac asked his father about the lamb. Abraham answered, "God himself will provide the lamb for the burnt offering."

Your life is no exception. What God has done for others, He will do for you, too. Begin to pronounce the following, and so shall it be.

Affirmation

Jehovah-Jireh is my provider.

WEEK 8

Wait for God's Timing

The Lord's timing is perfect. The Bible declares in Ecclesiastes 3:1, "There is a time for everything, and a season for every activity under the heavens." Sometimes we want to know if we are on the right path. We wonder if we have missed something along the way. We are still learning to walk with God. This must always be our first priority.

The Lord knows what He is doing. We may not, and we need to know to draw closer to Him when we sense negative thoughts and emotions creeping in. We must always remember that we are called apart. We are not to respond to every whim of our mind, will, and emotions. So many things God tries to teach us as our human nature flails about.

The children of Israel journeyed in the wilderness for forty years. During this time, they lacked nothing. Scripture says the Lord rained down manna from heaven for them. Today we have Jesus Christ, the bread of heaven. He has come in the flesh; He has called us to be His children and to learn to trust Him in the midst of our wilderness experiences.

Day by day and week by week, month after month and year after year we have new opportunities to learn how to follow God's instructions. There are so many riches of God's Word for us to learn during career transitions. Take time to enter into them. The danger is in thinking we can navigate the terrain leaning on our own understanding.

As we all travel this journey together in the fellowship of God's sons and daughters, may we learn to be still and know that He is God.

Ecclesiastes 3:1 Exodus 16:4 John 6:31–33
Proverbs 3:5–6 Psalm 46:10 Exodus 13:21

Let Us Reason Together

The Lord led the children of Israel by a pillar of cloud by day and a pillar of fire by night. Today He leads us by His Holy Spirit. He fed the children of Israel manna. Today He feeds us the Word of God. We grow by faith in Jesus Christ and in our relationship with Him. In our journey there are times of moving, and times of waiting, but we are always changing, growing in Him because He dwells within.

We are in a season of change as long as we are pilgrims and strangers here in this world. Allow the Lord to draw you to Himself and make the necessary changes He desires to make in you in order to conform you to the image of Christ as you allow God to work in your circumstances. Assert into your life the following and so shall it be.

Affirmation

My season of change is here!

SECTION TWO

Watch Out for Negative Emotions

WEEK 9

Keeping Hope Alive

Sometimes it can be so tempting to give up when you feel you have exhausted every option. But remember that you are on a path the Lord has crafted just for you. He has formed you in your mother's womb. You are the apple of His eye. He never loses sight of you. This is difficult for us to understand unless you realize that every trial we experience is designed to teach us how to trust and develop faith.

Remember to keep first things first. You are called to be a disciple and to make disciples. This means learning to walk in this world without falling prey to its snares and being led astray by all the many voices surrounding you. That is why in order to remain hopeful you must stay focused on following single mindedly the path he has laid out for you. This requires hope.

And where does hope come from? Your hope comes from the Lord who made heaven and earth (Psalm 121:1, NKJV). Let knowing that He has His eyes on you remind you to keep your mind on Him and on His Word, because He has told us that He has, "given us all things that pertain to life and godliness through the knowledge of Him" (2 Peter 1:3).

Jeremiah 1:5 Psalm 17:8 Isaiah 26:3 Psalm 123:1–2
Proverbs 7:2 2 Peter 1:3 Psalm 121:1 Hebrews 11:6

Let Us Reason Together

In Mark 5:21–40, Jairus asks Jesus to come heal his daughter who is at the point of death. On the way there, He heals the woman with the issue of blood. By the time He got to Jairus's house, He was told the daughter had already died. But this was no problem for Jesus.

"Don't be afraid; just believe," Jesus said to the father of the dead girl (verse 36). And He healed her. Over and over our faith will be tested, but our faith is being developed. Do you struggle with hopelessness in the time of crisis? Declare the following into your life, and open yourself up to God's miracles for your life.

Affirmation

No matter what is going on, I will not lose sight of hope.

WEEK 10

Beset by Anxiety and Fear

I don't know about you, but often my career situations have caused me a lot of anxiety and fear—either managing people to trying to break through on projects or in a career change situation. This is unscriptural but true. However, in these crippling situations, I became very intentional about my faith and began to confess the Word of God into my spirit:

> When you pass through the waters,
> I will be with you;
> and when you pass through the rivers,
> they will not sweep over you.
> When you walk through the fire,
> you will not be burned;
> the flames will not set you ablaze.
> For I am the LORD, your God,
> the Holy one of Israel, your Savior;
>
> —Isaiah 43:2–3

For the reader of this devotion, if you are struggling with the emotions of fear and anxiety in your career situation, I encourage you to get intentional about this fear and address it with the Word of God, which never lies or changes.

Fear cripples, but the Word of God gives us great assurance: "So do not fear, for I am with you; do not be dismayed, for I am your God. I will strengthen you and help you; I will uphold you with my righteous right hand" (Isaiah 41:10).

2 Timothy 1:7 Luke 12:32 Psalm 34:7
Deuteronomy 13:4

Let Us Reason Together

Consider turning your fear into praise when you feel oppressed with negative emotions such as anxiety and fear. Hold onto the promises of God in His Word, and proactively fight the spirit of fear in your career situation by declaring the following affirmation.

Affirmation

I will not be afraid!

WEEK 11

Anxiety Is the Enemy's Trap

Anxiety is another scheme of the enemy to try to get you off track and into the path of destruction or into a vulnerable position where he can attack. But the Lord's plan is to strengthen you and mature you and make you more useful for His kingdom. Always remember this.

God strengthens and matures you through trials and difficulties. You are His child. You are not just some average individual, which, of course, is what the enemy wants you to think. But there is nothing average about you if you are a child of God. You possess everything Jesus Christ possesses, and He intends to use you for His glory.

Day by day, week by week, month by month, and year by year, by the grace of God, you are growing more and more into conformity to the image of Christ. This is God's plan for your life. And this requires trust. We grow in trust too as we believe more and more what He has given us in His Word, because it is "alive and active. Sharper than any double-edged sword…" (Hebrews 4:12).

Hebrews 4:12 Nehemiah 9:6 Romans 4:18–19
Psalm 51:10

Let Us Reason Together

Think about Who it is you serve. Who is your Father? Think about this One who holds the heaven and the earth together in His hands, knows everything, has purchased you with the blood of Christ, and now offers you new life.

"You alone are the LORD," we read in Nehemiah 9:6. "You made the heavens, even the highest heavens, and all their starry host, the earth and all that is in it, the seas and all that is in them. You give life to everything, and the multitudes of heaven worship you."

The promises of God are yes and amen. Abraham believed and thus received the promise. Romans 4:18-19 says, "Against all hope, Abraham in hope believed and so became the father of many nations, just as it had been said to him, 'So shall your offspring be.' Without weakening in his faith, he faced the fact that his body was as good as dead—since he was about a hundred years old—and that Sarah's womb was also dead." God is able to supernaturally intervene in your situation and turn your life around. In the Bible, He did it for Esther, Joseph, and Daniel, and He will do it for you too.

Are you struggling with wavering faith because of a crisis you face? The Bible says in Psalm 51:10, "Create in me a pure heart, O God, and renew a steadfast spirit within me." Declare the following, and God will help you.

Affirmation

My heart is steadfast!

WEEK 12

Give All Shame to God

Shame is defined as "painful emotion caused by the awareness of having done something wrong or foolish."

Shame in our lives nullifies the fulfillment of God's purpose. Romans 10:11 declares, "Anyone who believes in him will never be put to shame."

I don't know about you, but I have made foolish choices in my career journey that have caused me great shame. One that comes to mind is allowing my emotions to take over my judgment and lead me to resign a job prematurely. I was certain it was God's plan for me to change careers (because He came through at the appropriate time, which led to the glorification of His name), but He wanted me to be patient for His appointed time, not mine, and I was not. As a result, I suffered the consequences of my foolish action and this led to shame in my life.

For the reader of this week's devotion, don't do what I did and bring unnecessary shame upon your life. I encourage you to be patient, trust God, don't lean on your own understanding, and wait for His appointed time for your career decisions—whether you are a seasoned professional trying to start a new business, change jobs or accept a promotion, or a student trying to get into the job market.

God's timing is always right. He is never too late, and He will show up for you at the appointed time.

Jeremiah 17:13 Psalms 25:2 Psalms 69:19

Let Us Reason Together

Are you losing sight of what God can accomplish in your life and the lives of others around you as you go through your career journey? I encourage you to seek God's face on what your next move should be, and wait patiently for the fulfillment of your prayers so that Hs name will be glorified in the final outcome.

Make the following declaration into your life, and so shall it be.

Affirmation

I will not be put to shame!

WEEK 13

Weariness Is Not a Part of God's Plan

Weariness. Everyone experiences it. And the Bible has a lot to say about it too. Words never stand alone. They always have their mental and emotional associations attached to them, which become a part of our thinking, and thus a part of our action. What does the word "weary" or "weariness" remind you of?

I just think of my Nana, my mother's mother, who came to the United States from Southampton, England, the year I was born. She did not complain about being weary; I just felt many times that she must have been weary because she was such an incredible servant. I guess I took for granted how much she worked to keep house, to cook food, to make cookies for us.

Some of my most precious memories are of sitting down to eat dinner after church on Sunday and of drying dishes with her afterwards, of having tea and Welsh cakes in the afternoon or the wonderful almond sugar cookies she made. How grateful we all should be of God's servants in this world, and is that not what we are on our jobs today? Be assured that God will provide you a place to serve as you diligently search.

In the *Strong's Concordance,* the word used for "weary" in Genesis 27:46 is *quwts* (pron. *koots*). Looking at this word and the words related to it, we have the idea of being disgusted, anxious, distressed, and grieved as well as "severing oneself from" something and to "loathe self." Many people struggle with what today is commonly called "low self-esteem." Recognize this is not God's plan for you. Remember, He is for you (Romans 8:31).

"Do not grow weary in doing good," Paul wrote to the Thessalonians (2 Thessalonians 3:13 NKJV).

Genesis 27:46 Romans 8:31 2 Thessalonians 3:13

Let Us Reason Together

When you are tired from working, traveling, looking for work, moving to a new situation, or any other activity that is physically or mentally draining, remember what Jesus said.

"Come to me, all you who are weary and burdened, and I will give you rest" (Matthew 11:28). Receive this word and practice it all week. God has given us more than we need or deserve. Are you grateful for His generosity?

Weariness is a tactic of the enemy to burn you out, slow you down, destroy your initiative, and discourage you from doing what God is calling you to do. Fight weariness by standing firm and declaring the following.

Affirmation

I will not grow weary!

WEEK 14

Change Defeat into Victory

Are you excelling in your career? Joshua took over from Moses and excelled. As a result, God told him, "Today I will begin to exalt you in the eye of all Israel, so that they may know I am with you as I was with Moses" (Joshua 3:7).

The scripture in Mark 11:23 confirms that you too can excel in your career journey. All you need to do is exercise your faith. "Truly I tell you, if anyone says to this mountain, 'Go, throw yourself into the sea,' and does not doubt in their heart but believes that what they say will happen, it will be done for them."

The above scripture can revolutionize your career path and change defeat into victory. What does it tell you? Your "mountain" may be your great career challenge (employer, employee relationships, the lack of promotion, the situations that lead to playing politics with people's lives, the disappointing performance appraisals and the back-stabbing situations to get ahead in the work place).

Or it could be that you are currently unemployed and trying to get work; or you are in transition from one career change to another. Whatever that situation may be for you this week, your "mountain"—that tremendous barrier—can be broken down and ousted from your life.

You must not doubt "in your heart." Allow no negative thoughts to exist in your subconscious mind. Pray that your mountainous difficulty shall be removed, and, as you pray, believe that it is being done then and now.

Psalm 27:1 Matthew 6:10 *Joshua 3:7*

Let Us Reason Together

Are you excelling in your career and overwhelmed by the goodness of God in your life? If yes, the best witness happens when your heart is full of appreciation for that God has done.

If no, this week you are able to change your career mountain by looking at it from a different perspective. Begin to make the following declaration into your life, and so shall it be.

Affirmation

I am anointed to excel in every area of my life!

SECTION THREE

Dealing With Difficult Situations

WEEK 15

Trusting God in Difficulty

> "For I know the plans I have for you," declares the LORD, "plans to prosper you and not to harm you, plans to give you hope and a future. Then you will call on me and come and pray to me, and I will listen to you. You will seek me and find me when you seek with all your heart. I will be found by you," declares the LORD, "and will bring you back from captivity. I will gather you from all the nations and places where I have banished you," declares the LORD, "and will bring you back to the place from which I carried you into exile."
>
> —Jeremiah 29:11–14

"You will seek me and find me when you seek me with all your heart" (verse 13), is a promise, as well as the promise of plans to prosper you and not to harm you and plans to give you hope and a future (verse 11). Verse 11 is often quoted, and we are tempted to look to the plans of prosperity and the hope for the future and somehow miss the point of the ultimate plan, hope, and future, which is to seek the Lord with all your heart.

First Chronicles 29:12 (NKJV) declares: "Both riches and honor come from You, and You reign over all." Jesus taught us we cannot serve both God and mammon. May our motives always be the will of God, the glory of God, directed by the love of God.

Jeremiah 29:11–14 1Chronicles 29:12
Matthew 6:24 Luke 16:13

Let Us Reason Together

Trusting God is a key part of your faith. The Bible says in Hebrews 11:6, "And without faith it is impossible to please God, because anyone who comes to him must believe that he exists and that he rewards those who earnestly seek him." Has your trust in God wavered in a time of crisis?

As you declare this week's affirmation, believe and trust God for the best as He works His wonders through you!

Affirmation

The works of my hands are blessed!

WEEK 16

The Sorrow of Betrayal

Among many definitions, sorrow is defined as, "sad, unhappy, regretful and downcast." Naomi (who is recorded in the Bible in the lineage of our Lord Jesus Christ) experienced great sorrow in her life, and it had a profound effect on her. When she returned to her hometown, we read of her reaction: "Don't call me Naomi," she told them. "Call me Mara, because the Almighty has made my life very bitter" (Ruth 1:20).

Naomi was expressing her pain through the heartbreaking events she had endured. Are you, like Naomi, going through sorrow because of betrayal from your current career situation or sorrowful because of the lack of opportunity for future opportunities and growth?

Your attitude during the period of waiting for the manifestation of your prayers is very crucial to God. You must learn how to conduct yourself, recognizing that negative situations will not bow to your attitude, but a choice to shift from sorrow to praise will transform your situation. It does not matter how much trouble you are facing, provided you keep on praying. God will be there to make sure you have a great testimony in the end.

The moment you see the appearance of an unpleasant situation, go immediately to your closet and begin to call on the Almighty God.

Psalm 50:15 Philippians 2:27 Psalms 34:18

Let Us Reason Together

Crises! Crises! Crises! One crisis seems to follow another, doesn't it? At least that is the appearance when you are feeling sorrowful. Can you recall a time in your life when you felt sorrowful and hopeless but God supernaturally intervened? Calling to remembrance these moments will help you put things in perspective.

This week make a choice to reject sorrow in every area of your life by confessing the following, and experience transformation from within.

Affirmation

I refuse to be sorrowful!

WEEK 17

Turning Failure into Godly Success

Why does the Lord let us fail? Did He not promise that for the one who delights in His law and meditates therein, "whatever he does shall prosper" (Psalms 1:1–3, NKJV)? Likewise in Joshua 1:8 (NKJV) we read: "This Book of the Law shall not depart from your mouth, but you shall meditate in it day and night, that you may observe to do according to all that is written in it. For then you will make your way prosperous, and then you will have good success."

Here are a few things to consider as we think about this issue of failure in the life of a Christian. I think the first one is that our definition of success must surely be different than God's. We know that the Word exhorts us not to love the world or the things that are in the world (1 John 2:15–17). And we know that in the world, success basically means fame and/or fortune or at least being at the top of your game in whatever career you choose.

But God's Word tells us that we are to serve God, not mammon (Matthew 6:24). So, first of all, consider that the career you worked so long to achieve just may not be God's ultimate plan for your life. You may then ask, "Why did the Lord let me fail in this career?" Or, "why did He not give me that job? I thought the Lord enabled me to pass all those courses, write all those papers, do all that research, and yet, the career did not work out. I had a great interview. I thought surely they would offer me the job." Surely, that is a great disappointment, but does that mean you have failed? Only if you fail in your response to this event.

I have heard plenty of messages on moral failure, but I have never heard a message on career failure. I finally found a list of possible reasons. At the top of the list consider the question Jesus asked Peter in John 21:15: "Simon son of Jonah, do you love Me more than these?"

When Simon Peter answered him, "Yes, Lord: You know I love You," Jesus said, "Tend My sheep." So this is the first and most important point to remember. We who have been called to be disciples of Jesus have been called to trust the Lord wherever He leads us, because we have given Him the Lordship of our lives. We are no longer the lord of our lives. So, we are called simply to trust in Him and not to our own understanding, as we know from Proverbs 3:5–6.

The Lord is much more interested in our success as a disciple than He is in our success the way the world views success. He is looking for ambassadors for Christ in the workplace as well as on the mission field. Or you might say your job is your mission field. Here are some additional benefits to receive in the process of failing to be successful by the world's definition. You will learn to:

- Have compassion (2 Corinthians 1:3-4)
- Be content (Philippians 4:11; Hebrews 13:5)
- Trust in God's broader plan (Proverbs 16:9)
- Love God more than this world. (1 John 2:15–17; Philippians 1:9; 3:10)
- Value Christ's priorities (Matthew 6:33; 2 Corinthians 2:14)
- Accept circumstances as a means to greater usefulness (Philippians 1:12)
- Develop humility (Philippians 2:7–8)
- Develop greater trust in God, less in self (2 Corinthians 1:9)

- Be grateful (Philippians 4:8; Ephesians 5:20; 1 Thessalonians 5:18)

Let Us Reason Together

Can any good thing come out of your crisis situation? What are some good things that have already come out of your crisis that will help you cope right now? In your crisis, refuse to fail. Declare the following affirmation into your life, and experience victory in Jesus.

Affirmation

I will not fail!

WEEK 18

Surrender Your Frustrations

Do you feel you have given your career path your best—worked hard, gone to school and received all the degrees, certification, and designation to show for it, rose on the corporate ladder, established your own business? You know what I mean. You have done all that it takes to be successful, and you are still left with a feeling of frustration?

I recently found out that the Bible classifies success into good success and negative or bad success. To the carnal mind, the idea of a bad success is ironic. The Lord defined the type of success that emanates from Him in Proverbs 10:22 as, "The blessing of the LORD brings wealth, without painful toil for it."

To the reader of this devotion, I encourage you this week to surrender your career journey and decisions to the Lord. Ask Him to give you His best for your life, let Him teach you and show you His mercy. Above all, let Him fill you with the spirit of intelligence and wisdom to make the right choices in your career path. It will save you from a lot of frustrated choices and decisions.

God takes pride in us coming to Him and asking, "What shall I do in this situation, Lord?" First John 5:14 affirms that, "This is the confidence we have in approaching God: that if we ask anything according to his will, he hears us."

You should be encouraged by this scripture and approach His throne with confidence for your career needs.

One of my favorite scriptures that has encouraged me in my career journey is Isaiah 40:31: "Those who hope in the LORD will renew their strength. They will soar on wings like eagles; they will run and not grow weary, they will walk and not be faint."

Proverbs 9:10 Daniel 12:4 Job 5:13

Let Us Reason Together

We need intelligence and wisdom to navigate any career situation we face. Do you remember Daniel? The Bible tells us that God honored him by sending a messenger to him, because he humbled himself. Daniel 10:12 records this event.

Do not be afraid, Daniel. Since the first day that you set your mind to gain understanding and to humble yourself before your God, your words were heard, and I have come in response to them.

State the following into your life, and let God fill you with confidence.

Affirmation

I am filled with the spirit of intelligence and wisdom!

WEEK 19

Believe for Greater Things

God does extraordinary things through the lives of ordinary people. Journey with me this week to the Book of Judges, chapter 6, verse 14, and look at the life of Gideon. The verse reads, "The Lord turned to him and said, 'Go in the strength you have and save Israel out of Midian's hand. Am I not sending you?'"

For the reader of this week's devotion, the awesomeness of God's power should cause you to totally rely on Him for your career journey. Think about Him as the One who created this journey in the first place, the One who owns the knowledge and wisdom of this world and is able to guide your steps to good success.

In the midst of all career uncertainty, I encourage you to appreciate and thank God for the past, present, and future, because He knows about them, and you don't.

Just as God took an ordinary man like Gideon and made him extraordinary, He can do the same for you. Imagine what you think is impossible, and start praying to the God of possibilities to make it possible.

I encourage you this week to stretch your faith. Keep a prayer journal and watch God amaze you.

In my career journey, I would write out my prayer requests and daily pray and thank God for the answers. Over the course of time, I have revisited this prayer journal, and since 2015 have seen how God has indeed transformed my situation.

My relationship and history with God have allowed me to continue to believe Him for greater things, because I believe God answers prayers.

Numbers 23:19 Isaiah 65:24 Psalm 66:19

Let Us Reason Together

Your life must be extraordinary in order to show off God's glory. Consider some of the things you could do to improve in this area and back it up with action and confession of the following affirmation, and you will be honored.

Affirmation

I will be extraordinary!

WEEK 20

God Carries Your Burdens

My friends, there is one fundamental truth you should depend on to successfully walk your career journey, and that truth is, you are precious in God's eyes.

Psalm 8:4 (NAS) states, "What is man that You take thought of him, and the son of man that You care for him?"

God loves you so much that He sent His Son to die for you on the cross of Calvary, and if that does not make you precious, I don't know what will.

A human mind can stand only so much weight. One mental burden piled upon another, unless relief is obtained, will in due course cause you to reach your breaking point and cause serious difficulty. Fortunately, you do not need to carry your burdens without assistance. God will help you to carry your career burden because you are precious in His eyes. But how is this done? It is accomplished in the mind.

Practice thinking that God is actually with you and loves you. Tell Him about your career burdens, and believe that He relieves and assists you. Form a picture of yourself as shifting your burdens to Him. He is willing to assume them and is perfectly able to do so. But, and this is most important, don't half give them. And don't take them back.

This week start celebrating the love of Christ for you. Know that He knitted you together in your mother's womb and that you are fearfully and wonderfully made. Be encouraged that His plans for you are plans of good and not of evil.

Psalms 139:13–16 Ephesians 2:4–9
Jeremiah 29:11

Let Us Reason Together

What can we learn from the Book of Job? Scripture says that Job was a man of faith, patience, and endurance. From Job's life you can learn that challenging times are not always a punishment from God. Let this reassure you as you journey through your career this week.

Take hold of God's great love for you and confess the following into your life.

Affirmation

I am precious in God's eyes

WEEK 21

Armor Up to "Stand" Against Afflictions

What does it mean to be afflicted? It means to be in a state of pain, distress, or misery.

I would say a majority of us in our career situations have felt one or more of these emotions, either through being overworked or unappreciated or in office or business politics. The effect of these situations has not only left us miserable, but also sometimes in a state of pain.

Naaman, a great commander of the army of the king of Aram, suffered a grievous affliction. Second Kings 5:1 reveals that, "... he was a valiant soldier, but he had leprosy."

When I have felt afflicted in my career journey, Ephesians 6:13 has brought comfort to my soul. "Therefore, put on the full armor of God, so that when the day of evil comes, you may be able to stand your ground, and after you have done everything, to stand."

This scripture is one of the greatest techniques of mental health. It teaches that when we have done all that we can do about a given situation, we are not to get worried or in a panic or be filled with anxiety, but take a calm, philosophical attitude concerning it.

When you have done all that you can do, don't try to do any more, just "stand." Relax, stop, be quiet, don't fuss about it; you have done everything possible, leave the results to God.

Naaman did all he could do and did not even believe his healing could come from an ordinary river, but eventually he left the outcome of the situation to God and was cured of leprosy.

Nahum 1:9 Psalm 34:19 2 Corinthians 1:4

Let Us Reason Together

Which of your career dreams, goals, and aspirations has not yet been realized? The Scriptures record that God knew you before you were formed in your mother's womb (Isaiah 44:2, 24; 49:5). This knowledge gives great hope that your dreams will one day come to pass.

Arise and begin to declare the following, and God will deliver you from your career afflictions.

Affirmation

I will not suffer any affliction!

WEEK 22

Disappointment Needs a Steadfast Spirit

Life is full of many, many disappointments. Usually these disappointments are born out of frustration. However, the key is to remain faithful in your frustrations.

None of us are exempt from our career path often being paved with expected and unexpected frustrations. However, we have an opportunity to take these disappointments and turn them into divine appointments.

How, you might ask? Psalm 51:10 is the answer.

> Create in me a pure heart, O God, and renew a steadfast spirit within me.

This scripture will bring you happiness and success in your career path. It can improve your disposition. The quality of your disposition depends upon your inner spirit. The use of the word "renew" implies that when you were created, you had a good disposition.

Your career journey may have allowed your good disposition to deteriorate, but the almighty God who created you can recreate and renew in you the fine balance and controlled spirit you need to face career and financial challenges. He can restore that vital factor of a good disposition and inner quiet control you need to endure pressure brought about by these stressors.

Throughout this week ask God to renew a right spirit within you and to give you the anointing to turn all your career disappointments into appointments.

Romans 5:5 Romans 10:11 Psalm 51:10

Let Us Reason Together

God wants us to cast our cares and burden on Him. Why continue to bear them if we say we trust Him? Arise in your spirit and begin to refuse the spirit of disappointment. Confess the following and so shall it be.

Affirmation

I will not be disappointed!

SECTION FOUR

Struggling for Promotion

God's View of Greatness

Greatness is not the word that immediately comes to mind when you are unemployed, in a job looking for a new job, or in a career transition.

This is because the world's view of greatness and the Lord's view of greatness reflect completely different perspectives.

Let's focus on God's view of greatness as you navigate through your career path this week. The Word of God reminds us in Philippians 4:13 that you can do all things through Christ who strengthens you. This scripture speaks of God's ability to do great and mighty things through you this week as you send out your resumes, follow a job lead, or interview for a job.

You just have to tap into His greatness and ask Him to give you the wisdom, knowledge, and understanding you need. Proverbs 3:19–20 declares that, "By wisdom the LORD laid the earth's foundation, by understanding he set the heavens in place; by his knowledge the deeps were divided, and the clouds let drop the dew."

For the reader of this devotion, I know He will share His greatness, wisdom, knowledge, and understanding with you.

Jeremiah 10:6 (NASB) 1 Chronicles 16:25
Psalms 96:4

Let Us Reason Together

When the Lord does not show up when you need Him this week, is it appropriate to question Him? Or just keep on seeking His face.

Using the following affirmation, confess your greatness (through Christ) and watch Him show His greatness in your life this week.

Affirmation

I am destined for greatness!

WEEK 24

Career Journey Opportunities

Isaiah 43:19 says, "See, I am doing a new thing! Now it springs up; do you not perceive it? I am making a way in the wilderness and streams in the wasteland."

My personal experience when I was changing careers led to self-doubt and constantly struggling to maintain a positive attitude. This mindset is unproductive and drains you emotionally. Romans 12:2 says, "Do not conform to the pattern of this world, but be transformed by the renewing of your mind. Then you will be able to test and approve what God's will is—his good, pleasing and perfect will"

Rather than see this career journey as a crisis situation, begin to see it as an opportunity for the Lord to do a new thing in your life—to broaden your horizon, promote you, and help you find fulfillment in your next goal.

Let the Lord know you are trusting and believing that He, Jehovah, will do you good. Let your soul find rest in God alone, and let your hope come from Him. He alone is your Rock and Salvation; your Fortress and you will not be shaken. Your salvation and your honor depend on God; He is your Mighty Rock and Refuge (Psalms 6:5–7).

John 4:14 Isaiah 55:1 Jeremiah 31:25 Psalms 6:5–7

Let Us Reason Together

Does knowing that God is your Father help you cope as you journey through your career change? When your heart is troubled—which will happen because you are chronically human—assert the following, and it shall come to pass in your life.

Affirmation

New things are springing up in my life!

WEEK 25

Promotion Comes From the Lord

Insecurity, inadequacy, and devaluation of talent are some of the emotions that come with the territory of job search, being passed over for a promotion, facing a struggling or failed business.

These emotions, if not put under check, are crippling and could potentially ruin your hopes of fulfilling your destiny in your career goal.

Let me challenge you this week as you ponder this week's devotion to seek your comfort in Zion. Psalm 75:6 (KJV) states: "For promotion cometh neither from the east, nor from the west, nor from the south."

I personally have held onto this scripture and reminded God to show up on my behalf when I have experienced injustice in the workplace or have seen other people being dealt with the hands of injustice.

Friends, your promotion only comes from the Lord. He is the Alpha and Omega, and everything in our lives (including our career goals) centers on Him. He is able to turn around all the negative emotions we discussed earlier for your good. Scriptures often remind us that when we are weak, He is strong.

Psalms 92:10 Psalms 148:14 Psalms 75:10
2 Corinthians 12:10

Let Us Reason Together

Everyone is a prophet of his or her own destiny. Psalm 92:10 says, "You have exalted my horn like that of a wild ox; fine oils have been poured on me."

Declare into your life the following, and expect divine exaltation.

Affirmation

My horn is exalted like that of a wild ox.

WEEK 26

Grounded in the Vine for Growth

There are times when the demands of the day can cause us to have to take a backseat to our relationship with the Lord. When we are running and working and do not take time to feed on God's Word and rest in His presence, we will suffer for it. Can you imagine a flock of sheep running around all day and never stopping to eat or drink? We may be surrounded by machinery and electronics, but we are not robots.

Our affirmation for this week is that we will be like "well-nurtured plants" (Psalm 144:12). Something very interesting about plants is that they stay in one place—namely, in the ground. That is unless they are constantly being repotted, which may be the case with many of us. But in a spiritual sense, the Lord does desire for us to be "rooted and established in love" (Ephesians 3:17) and in our faith (Colossians 1:23).

Growing in love and faith requires time feeding on the things of God. We tend to think of this in terms of chores, tasks, to-do lists, and how-to instructions. When we do this, we get bound up in a works mentality and lose our joy and peace, without which we cannot function at our best.

"I am the vine; you are the branches. If a man remains in me and I in him, he will bear much fruit; apart from me you can do nothing," Jesus said to his disciples. So we see again the metaphor of a plant. Even with the metaphor of lambs and sheep there is the element of walking and running, but with the vine, we see the emphasis on remaining and receiving—abiding.

Psalm 144:12 Ephesians 3:17 Colossians 1:23
John 15:5–8

Let Us Reason Together

This week let the Lord teach you to receive from Him. He is not a genie in a bottle that we rub a certain way and He comes out and gives us what we wish for. He is God Almighty. And yet He is our Father through faith in His Son Jesus Christ. He offers us abundant life in Him.

Let the hand of the Lord be upon you as it was upon Ezekiel when He led him to the middle of a valley of dry bones! Maybe you feel like you're in a valley of dry bones this week.

> Then he [the Lord] said to me, "Prophesy to these bones and say to them, 'Dry bones, hear the word of the LORD! This is what the Sovereign LORD says to these bones: I will make breath enter you, and you will come to life."
>
> —Ezekiel 37:4–5

When plants are nurtured, they are beautiful and bring forth fruit, but when they are neglected they become dry and lifeless. You are not destined to lose life, but to bring forth your potential—what God can do with what He put in you! Begin to make the following declaration into your life, and so shall it be.

Affirmation

I will be like a well-nurtured plant.

WEEK 27

God Will Enlarge Your Territory

Remember Jabez? In 1 Chronicles 4:10, he prayed, "Oh that you would bless me and enlarge my territory. Let your hand be with me, and keep me from harm so that I will be free from pain."

This week, remind yourself that nothing is too good to be true. Your great hopes can be realized, and God can indeed enlarge your territory.

I share this testimony to the glory of God and to give you hope for your desired testimony.

Over three years ago my personal situation changed, and I moved to another town, which increased my commute to work from ten minutes to four hours a day. For over a year and a half I traveled one hundred fifty miles a day to work three days a week. My employer agreed to allow me to work from home two days a week to offset my commute. The three-day commute became unbearable, and I began to seek the face of the Lord to make a way where there seemed to be no way.

The Lord promised an open door for me, and yes, two job opportunities presented themselves for which I was recommended. I interviewed for these jobs and was convinced that God promised and He will bring it to pass. However, the two jobs did not come to fruition, and I was devastated. I began to question the Lord, and deep in my spirit I was reminded that if the Lord said He would open doors He would do so in His own timing.

While I was very discouraged, I kept believing God for an opportunity that would allow me to work out of my home office so I can serve Him and have quality of life.

The Lord began to align situations in my life to prepare me for this testimony. Unexpectedly, my employer called me and said that my role requires that I be in the office five days a week. This situation was indeed an answer to prayers.

I tendered my resignation and promised my employer that I would make sure I transitioned my role appropriately, giving them nearly two months' notice. Doing this gives God the glory because in whatever we do, we are to be a light in darkness and always shine for Jesus.

The same week I tendered my resignation (not knowing how the Lord would work this situation out), I got a call from a potential employer who believed that my skill sets were very much in line with what they were looking for.

From this call came a new job offer. The miracle of the job is not the job itself but rather what I thought would be impossible—the opportunity to work from home full-time. The Lord did it for me, and He can do it for you too.

1 Samuel 15:29 Joshua 24:15 Proverbs 3:5–6

Let Us Reason Together

What are you doing to prepare for your season of career change? The Lord granted Jabez his request. As you declare the following, your request shall be granted.

Affirmation

My territory is enlarged.

SECTION FIVE

The Christian's Business Relationships

WEEK 28

Believe in Yourself First

In your career journey, have you ever felt like you are not winning with colleagues in your job setting, or as a business owner that your team is not cutting the mustard, or, even worse, while you are unemployed you continue to send out resumes yet seem to have more rejection emails than interviews?

I have lived each of the seasons above, and often in each of these seasons I cried out to the Lord to show me mercy and wipe away my tears.

For the reader of this devotion who is feeling any of the emotions expressed above and thinking that your self-confidence is eroded and you are not destined to achieve any more than where you are currently, let me encourage you with words of wisdom from a mentor-friend many years ago that still resonate with me today.

> I should think every president of the United States wonders if he has what it takes as soon as he accepts the office (if you are not from the United States, apply this statement to the leader of your country), but he simply doesn't know.

When you are in this position, you have to rise to the occasion. The first thing you must do is to give yourself complete self-belief at the outset by saying to yourself that you are able to draw on many years of experience in (your field). Just remember, when you attain your career goal, you have no other choice but to redouble your efforts and redouble them again. You will then lead by example. It's lonely at the top, so make up your own mind whether this is something you really want![1]

Isaiah 3:10 1 Thessalonians 5:23 Romans 14:17

Let Us Reason Together

Think about the resources you need that will contribute to your future well-being and get you to your desired goal. Make up your mind to attain it. Declare the following affirmation into your life as you work toward this goal.

Affirmation

It is well with my body, soul, and spirit!

[1] Advice given from an actual conversation with a mentor.

WEEK 29

Put On Christ-like Characteristics

Many times on this journey to be conformed to the image of Christ and while seeking Him in order to know and do His will, we have to surrender our desires to Him—perhaps on a daily basis. Sometimes we seem to never measure up—either to our own expectations or the expectations of others. But, as in all trials of life, whom should we be seeking to please?

In the body of Christ, it seems we are most effective in relationships, even though this may provide challenges. While the people of the world strive for fame and popularity and to amass fortune for themselves, Christians seek to follow the leading of the Holy Spirit in every aspect of their lives for His ultimate glory, not their own. So we might expect, as imperfect creatures, to deal with our own failures and those of others from time to time.

The Bible gives us direction on this as on every other matter pertaining to life and godliness (2 Peter 1:3), if we will only seek His will.

"Therefore, as the elect of God, holy and beloved," Paul writes in Colossians 3:12–13 (NKJV), "Put on tender mercies, kindness, humility, meekness, longsuffering; bearing with one another, and forgiving one another, if anyone has a complaint against another; even as Christ forgave you, so you also must do."

After all, what are we most interested in as Christians in our lives? In following Jesus and making disciples, or in being popular with the world? Jesus came to take away the sins of the world (John 1:29). In Romans 8:37, Paul writes, "No, in all these things we are more than conquerors through him who loved us." If you look at the context you see He is talking about relationships:

"If God is for us, who can be against us?" (verse 31).

"Who will bring any charge against those whom God has chosen?" (verse 33).

"Who shall separate us from the love of Christ?" (verse 35).

"Since you are precious in My sight, you have been honored, and I have loved you; therefore I will give men for you, and people for your life," God spoke to Isaiah (Isaiah 43:4, NKJV). God's plan is for His body, not solely for individuals, and He has strategically placed you where He wants you to function. As you seek to follow Him and obey His commandments, He will bring you together with those He wishes for you to be a blessing to and those who will be a blessing to you. Don't let anything derail you from this path.

The Word tells us in 2 Corinthians 2:14 (NKJV) that God, "always leads us in triumph in Christ, and through us diffuses the fragrance of His knowledge in every place." What a privilege.

2 Peter 1:1-21 Colossians 3:1–25 John 1:1–51
Romans 8:1–37
Isaiah 431–28 2 Corinthians 2:14

Let Us Reason Together

When you are in a crisis, how do you see yourself? Do you see yourself as God sees you? Or are you so consumed with the situation that you only see and hear what the negative people around you are feeding back to you? "No, in all these things we are more than conquerors through him who loved us," Paul wrote in Romans 8:37. Affirm the following into your life, and so shall it be.

Affirmation

I am a conqueror!

WEEK 30

An Attitude Adjustment Takes a Renewed Mind

Have you ever heard of the phrase, "Attitude Adjustment"? I recall a time during my career journey, and even more recently, when I had to pray for an attitude adjustment because I focused on unpleasant situations at hand instead of the power of the God that I serve.

As you reflect on this week's devotion, let me encourage you with the scripture in Romans 12:2 (NKJV), which states: "And do not be conformed to this world, but be transformed by the renewing of your mind, that you may prove what is that good and acceptable and perfect will of God."

It is human to create our own unhappiness by the negative manner in which we think about things, and certainly ungodly to do this. Work with your mind—exercise disciplinary control and recreate your thoughts for happier living—even in your present career situation.

Picture your mind as completely empty, and start filling it with thoughts of God and of Christ's thoughts about every good and pleasant thing.

Ephesians 6:10–11 Philippians 4:8 Psalms 119:11 Philippians 2:5

Let Us Reason Together

It has been said that our attitude will determine our altitude. Ephesians 4:23 says, "Be made new in the attitude of your minds." Resolve today to align your thoughts and attitudes with God's will for your life by pronouncing the following affirmation.

Affirmation

My thoughts and attitudes are renewed!

WEEK 31

Your Purpose Will Affect Change in Others

Have you ever considered what your purpose in life is? Our ultimate purpose is to serve, worship, praise, and glorify God who created us. It is important not to lose sight of this because it is the foundation of being.

In the Old Testament, Joseph's purpose was to save his family from famine. Joseph's words to his brothers in Genesis 45:5 makes this clear. "And now, do not be distressed and do not be angry with yourselves for selling me here, because it was to save lives that God sent me ahead of you."

Just like Joseph, we are all products of His divine purpose. God has a general plan into which His specific plan for your life fits. You were created unique, one of a kind, and there can never be another you. The exact details of your life are in God's hands.

Your talents as a business owner, unemployed person, or employee are all part of your purpose to make a difference in the business environment. God is working in you and through you to be the best you can be in your career journey and effect change in your generation.

Proverbs 16:20 states, "Whoever gives heed to instruction prospers, and blessed is the one who trusts in the LORD."

Fulfilling your purpose and living successfully in your career journey requires overcoming blundering ineptness. It requires developing the deft and skillful touch that makes things turn out right. Things do not go wrong because of some perverse fate. It is more than likely that one lacks the right slant or the proper approach, and in such cases what is needed is wisdom. And wisdom comes from God (James 1:5).

Genesis 45:5 Ephesians 2:10 Isaiah 43:6–7
Psalm 86:12 James 1:5

Let Us Reason Together

Do you know why God made you? Have you keyed into the purpose of God for your life? Are you where God wants you to be and doing what He wants you to do in your career path?

Every one of us has been destined to walk out our purpose in life. However, we are often distracted by life's situations from accomplishing this. Declare into your life the following and so shall it be.

Affirmation

I will fulfill my purpose in life!

WEEK 32

Called to Good Works

The Lord wants us to be "a worker…who correctly handles the world of truth" (2 Timothy 2:15). Jesus said there would be false teachers (Matthew 7:15–23). And what better time could the enemy choose to lead you astray than when you are feeling down and discouraged about a career or a financial situation? The enemy is called our enemy for a reason.

Here are some scriptures that have helped me to stay focused on the Lord and not on my situation, and not get carried away by "every wind of teaching and by the cunning and craftiness of men in their deceitful scheming" (Ephesians 4:14). When we are unhappy in our employment or frustrated in our job search or ministry, it will be tempting to escape by any means.

Paul wrote to Timothy that the time would come when people would turn from the truth and hear what they want to hear (2 Timothy 4:3). The world may use alcohol, drugs, entertainment, gambling, or sex for escape. The Christian may look for spiritual highs or an illusion of significance or position offered by teachers with hidden agendas. Sadly, the agenda may even be hidden from the teachers themselves.

As a child of God, you are called to good works that glorify your Father (Matthew 5:14–16). Your primary job is to find out what those works are and do them, no matter what your position is in the work world.

Matthew 7:15–23 2 Timothy 2:15 Ephesians 4:14
2 Timothy 4:3 Matthew 5:14–16

Let Us Reason Together

Saul disobeyed God and lost His favor. In 1 Samuel 15:26, God, speaking through Samuel, said, "You have rejected the word of the Lord, and the Lord has rejected you as king over Israel." God had directed Saul to destroy the Amalekites and everything that belonged to them, but instead Saul spared Agag and the best of the sheep and the cattle.

Saul did things *his* way and tried to justify it to God. This did not work for Saul, and it will not work for us. Remember, partial obedience is disobedience. Instead, we want to walk in God's blessing and favor because of obedience, and be recipients of God's faithfulness, as the psalmist proclaims in Psalm 85:1–3:

> You, Lord, showed favor to your land;
> you restored the fortunes of Jacob.
> You forgave the iniquity of your people
> and covered all their sins.
> You set aside all your wrath
> and turned from your fierce anger.

Flee from anything that will cause you to walk in disobedience to God, and begin to declare the following in your life.

Affirmation

I will not walk in error!

SECTION SIX

The Provisions of God

WEEK 33

Wait Patiently for His Blessings

For the reader of this week's devotion, expect the Lord to bless your coming in and going out in this week regardless of your career situation.

I recall my own job search journey when there would be a glimmer of hope from a prospective employer's phone call, and even sometimes a phone interview, and then silence. These roller coaster emotions were often discouraging. However, I took comfort from the words of God in Deuteronomy 28:6, "You will be blessed when you come in and blessed when you go out."

The blessings of the Lord are not only measured in the outcome of your current career situation, it is all around you—in the opportunity to see a new day, the change of season, the roof over your head, the family, friends, and church community you have.

Proverbs 10:22 Numbers 6:24–26 Malachi 3:10

Let Us Reason Together

It is natural to respond with disappointment in the journey of unemployment and uncertain work situation. However, is it ungodly to feel a sense of hopelessness in such situations?

Consider starting the day off by committing your day into the hands of the Lord and confessing it! The Bible tells us in Deuteronomy 28:1–14 that if we fully obey the commandments of our God, many blessings will come upon us. There is power in the tongue. Affirm this power by claiming the following for your life this week, and so shall it be.

Affirmation

I am blessed in my going out and my coming in!

WEEK 34

God Is Ever Faithful

In the midst of my frustration, I give You praise for Your faithfulness and provision, Lord. You said the work of God was to believe in You, Jesus, whom God sent (John 6:29).

Thank You that I am alive, that I am working, even if I am looking for a job, if I have a part-time job, if I am receiving any form of income at all, and, yes, even if I am not. Thank You, Lord, for supernatural provision, for finances that come in from unexpected sources when they are right on time!

You said that You clothed the lilies and fed the birds, and You have provided for me every day as I seek first Your kingdom and Your righteousness (Matthew 6:33). Thank You that I am alive and able to shine the light of Christ wherever I go and whatever I do today.

How important it is to praise You at all times. This gives voice to the faith that is "the victory that overcomes the world," as the old song says!

> Praise the Lord, my soul;
>   all my inmost being, praise his holy name.
> Praise the Lord, my soul,

and forget not all his benefits—
who forgives all your sins
and heals all your diseases,
who redeems your life from the pit
and crowns you with love and compassion,
who satisfies your desires with good things
so that your youth is renewed like the eagle's.
—Psalm 103:1–5

Lord, how true are Your words! Give me a grateful heart.

John 6:29 Matthew 6:33 Psalm 103:1–5

Let Us Reason Together

Praising God in a time of crisis may be the hardest thing you try to do, yet it can be one of the most rewarding. How does allowing your emotions to rule over a situation cause you to be angry with God? How does praising Him get you back on track?

Isaiah 61:3 says, "To console those who mourn in Zion, to give them beauty for ashes, the oil of joy for mourning, the garment of praise for the spirit of heaviness; that they may be called trees of righteousness, the planting of the Lord, that He may be glorified."

With the following declaration, call joy into being in your life.

Affirmation

I am anointed with the oil of gladness!

WEEK 35

God's Peace in a Chaotic World

Look around your environment—be it business, geographically, locally, nationally, or internationally—and all you will see (through the physical eyes) is chaos.

This confusion also affects every facet of our day-to-day life, more so in the journey of our career path and change. From a personal experience, I too have felt helpless and desperate, and if we are not careful the enemy of our soul can use this opportune moment to cripple us emotionally, physically, and spiritually. His ultimate goal is to remind us of how inadequate we are, and to sometimes paint a picture of hopelessness.

In this journey we are reminded of God's words in Philippians 4:7 confirming that: "the peace of God, which transcends all understanding, will guard your hearts and your minds in Christ Jesus." Friends, this is our only assurance, and there is no greater promise than this.

Jesus makes all the difference in our lives, and He sticks closer than a brother. It is God's will for you to be at peace in every aspect of your life. One of the practical steps to bring about the peace of God into your life is through thanksgiving and worship.

John 14:27 John 16:33 John 20:19

Let Us Reason Together

There is a reader of this devotion who needs peace for this week. Begin to thank God for who He is in your life, worship Him because He is good, and stand against every peace stealer by pronouncing the following affirmation into your life.

Affirmation

I am at peace!

WEEK 36

Surrounded by God's Presence

Do you ever wonder why it's so difficult to remember that we are continuously surrounded and indwelt by the presence of God? The simplest answer to that may be that He is not necessarily perceptible to our senses, however, He may reveal himself in any of them.

People say they have actually heard God's audible voice, some have visions. Some even claim to have tasted or smelled a particular sweetness at times that they believed God meant as a special reminder of His presence. But most of the time most of us don't see, touch, or hear him, except in our spirits. We sometimes *feel* the presence of the Lord in our emotions, or a sense of physical well-being that will seem to overtake us like a shot of adrenalin or a boost of endorphins. There are many ways God has of connecting with his people.

We may say we hear Him in our *heart* or in our *gut*—some place inside of us different than our five senses—yet we say we *hear* what He is saying. This is possible because Jesus said, "My sheep hear My voice, and I know them, and they follow Me" (John 10:27, NKJV).

It is clear that God is very interested in developing our faith and our ability to hear His voice and know what His will is. The Bible is full of stories in which He is asking people to demonstrate their faith.

When Jesus had fallen asleep in the boat on the lake during a windstorm, and His disciples were panicked, Jesus asked His disciples the same question He asks us.

"Where is your faith?" (Luke 8:25, NKJV).

"Master. Master, we are perishing!" the disciples had said (verse 24). Is this not like us when we are in a crisis concerning employment? We are just like those disciples in the boat with Jesus. He is continually asking us to choose faith over fear.

So when you are turned down for a job or you lose a job, or you don't receive a call for an interview, why do you think God would allow this? Certainly not to crush you, but because you are His child and He desires to develop your faith, and He may want to talk to you about His direction for your life. He also wants you to evaluate where your faith is: Is it in yourself, in money, in a paycheck or a person, in a company, or in your own agenda for your life? Or are you seeking to trust Him completely in every aspect of your life?

He knows we have needs, as we learn in Matthew 6:24-34 (NKJV). But we cannot serve God and mammon (Matthew 6:24), Jesus said. Where do you think He wants our faith to be? In Him; nowhere else. And we will be tried in this matter.

Sometimes a disappointment will churn up feelings of anger or fear, which God wants us to address. And He has told us how to do that.

"If we confess our sins, He is faithful and just to forgive us our sins and to cleanse us from all unrighteousness" (1 John 1:9, NKJV). And then we move on in faith.

"Yea, though I walk through the valley of the shadow of death, I will fear no evil; for You are with me; Your rod and Your staff, they comfort me" (Psalms 23:4, NKJV). This is His promise to us. He will be with us to guide and comfort us.

John 10:27 Luke 8:24–25 Matthew 6:24–34
1 John 1:9
Psalms 23:4 Job:14 Isaiah 40:31

Let Us Reason Together

Job suffered great affliction, and as he did in Job 14:14, we too must declare, "I will wait for my renewal to come." The Bible encourages us to wait on the Lord so that we can renew our strength (Isaiah 40:31). As you confess the following, be renewed in the spirit of your mind (Ephesians 4:23, NKJV).

Affirmation

I will wait for my renewal to come.

WEEK 37

An Ever-Present Help

Remember Hannah in the Old Testament. The Lord turned her darkness into light. The Bible say in 1 Samuel 1:19 that, "...the Lord remembered her."

For the reader of this week's devotion, the Lord will remember you in your career journey.

When trouble strikes in your career journey—either your employer unexpectedly calls you in and hands you a pink slip, or as a business owner that contract you depend on suddenly gets canceled—what you want is comfort and protection. You want strength to stand up to the situation. Psalm 46:1 has often provided me great comfort in trying times like this: "God is our refuge and strength, an ever-present help in trouble."

A situation that comes to mind was during my bout with unemployment. I was in the process of a positive and encouraging interview process, and a couple of days later I received a phone call from the prospective employer indicating that the organization had decided to hold off on hiring for this position because of the economic crisis and market uncertainty.

Frequently remind yourself that God is with you, that He will never fail you, that you can count upon Him. New hope will flood your mind. New ideas will come. A new sense of power will be felt. As a result, you will move from a situational dark place into light.

Psalm 18:28 2 Corinthians 4:6 1 Peter 2:9

Let Us Reason Together

Are you able to express your feelings and talk about your career challenges with God? Or is your natural reaction to call all your friends first? Undoubtedly, you need friends, but God can help you gain the right perspective.

Declare into your life the following, and the Lord will change your situation for good.

Affirmation

My darkness will be turned to light.

WEEK 38

From Panic to Peace

This week we are going to turn our thoughts toward what God says about us in Scripture, about how we are "fearfully and wonderfully made" (Psalms 139:14). First of all, think how remarkable it is that He has given us His Spirit, the Holy Spirit, the third person of the Trinity, to live inside us. That is, God Himself has come to dwell in these "tents of flesh."

We are His "earthen vessels" with this treasure within, "that the excellence of the power may be of God and not of us" (2 Corinthians 4:7, NKJV). Whatever you may be good at, or whatever you are not good at, always remember God made you for a purpose, and He knows what that purpose is.

This may be a good time to read Psalms 139 in order to be reminded how much God cares about you. A few points may be useful here. Know that God:

1. Knows you and everything about you (verses 1–4)
2. Is with you wherever you go (verses 5–12)
3. Created you and has a plan for your life (verses13–16)
4. Is always thinking about you (verses 17–18)

In verses 19–22, David pours out his heart to God, the way we do when we are discouraged. "If only you, God, would slay the wicked" he cries. And don't we feel this way many times the closer we grow to God? This world is so foreign to us sometimes, and we feel small, insignificant, and powerless to change anyone or anything.

But in verses 23 and 24, David's heart is turned to his God as he pleads with Him, "Search me, O God, and know my heart; test me and know my anxious thoughts. See if there is any offensive way in me, and lead me in the way everlasting!" This is where God desires us to be with a heart after God, fully trusting in Him to work all things together for our good (Romans 8:28) and His glory.

Psalms 139 2 Corinthians 4:7 Romans 8:28

Let Us Reason Together

Your crisis situation may not look great right now, in your estimation. And you may be conditioned to panic during difficult trials. But God is never directing you to panic. Sometimes it takes literally the "twinkling of an eye" to get in touch with the peace of God. Other times it may take longer. The main thing is to turn to Him in faith.

What He wants to do through you He is able to do, but He wants to bless you with a deeper intimacy with Him and trust in Him. This is pretty clear in Scripture.

Paul pleaded with God to remove a thorn in the flesh; then God told him, "My grace is sufficient for you, for my power is made perfect in weakness" (2 Corinthians 12:8–9). Then Paul responded with: "That is why, for Christ's sake, I delight in weaknesses, in insults, in hardships, in persecutions, in difficulties. For when I am weak, then I am strong" (2 Corinthians 12:10). God transformed Paul from a persecutor of Christians into a preacher of the gospel.

What will you let Him do in your life? Assert the following into your life and rest in His love and care for you and His plan for your life.

Affirmation

I am fearfully and wonderfully made.

WEEK 39

Receive His Mercy

When you decided to live your life in utter dependence on the Lord, you had to resolve inwardly to trust in the mercy of God. You decided to trust in Him, "with all your heart and lean not on your own understanding; in all your ways submit to him, and he will make your paths straight" (Proverbs 3:5–6). No one else you know may be doing this, but you believe God has called you to present yourself to Him entirely for His purposes. And you have decided not to back down.

Think about it. You have to believe God is merciful in order to walk in this way. The enemy may lie to you and accuse you day and night (Revelation 12:10), intending to fill you full of fear and doubt, but don't listen.

Mercy, strictly speaking, is kindness and favor. In Genesis 43:14, Jacob prayed that God would grant his sons mercy before Joseph, who had requested they bring Benjamin, his youngest son. The word for mercy in this verse is *racham (rakh-am)* or compassion, and this word implies the *womb*.

Jacob trusted God so much when sending Benjamin with his brothers that he used the word for mercy that implies that God's mercy may be likened to the cherishing of a fetus by the womb! Now that is something to think about. This metaphor describes the love and compassion the Lord extends to us every day. He can be trusted!

Proverbs 3:5–6 Revelation 12:10 Psalm 23:6
Genesis 43:14

Let Us Reason Together

If you are not going through a crisis now you either will face one in the future or you have just come out of one. Thus you will be able to comfort someone else going through one (2 Corinthians 1:4)! Tribulation is in the world, but remember Jesus said to, "Be of good cheer, I have overcome the world" (John 16:33, NKJV). He makes a way for His own who are seeking His kingdom and His righteousness (Matthew 6:33).

"Those who sow with tears will reap with songs of joy," the psalmist wrote in Psalm 126:5.

"I lift up my eyes to the mountains—where does my help come from? My help comes from the LORD, the Maker of heaven and earth" (Psalm 121:1–2). May these victorious verses be your testimony this week.

"Surely goodness and mercy shall follow me all the days of my life," (Psalm 23:6, NKJV) the psalmist declares. Assert the following declaration in your life, and begin the life-changing experience of knowing God's mercy.

Affirmation

I receive mercy.

WEEK 40

Nothing Is Impossible

Here is an interesting point to consider: With God, nothing shall be impossible for us, the Bible says (Matthew 17:20; Mark 10:27; Luke 1:37; 18:27). But there are a couple of things that are impossible: Without faith it is impossible to please God! (Hebrews 11:6). And it is impossible for God to lie (Hebrews 6:18)! So whatever He speaks to you in His Word, whatever He illumines to your heart for your life according to His Word, is yours!

In view of the fact that without faith it is impossible to please God, and that it is impossible for God to lie, then it should be easier for us to believe that nothing shall be impossible for us who believe in Jesus. He has given us quite a few promises in this regard.

Paul wrote from the Philippian jail: "I can do all this through him who gives me strength." He said that he had "learned the secret of being content in any and every situation, whether well fed or hungry, whether living in plenty or in want" (Philippians 4:12–13).

In Philippians, Paul was referring to conditions he had experienced as he was doing what God called him to do for the cause of Jesus Christ. In Luke 1:37, the angel had just told Mary she would give birth to the Messiah, and she needed reassurance that with God nothing is impossible!

For us this is assurance that whatever God wants to do in our lives and whatever God is directing us to do, He is able to perform through us.

Matthew 17:20 Mark 10:27 Luke 1:37; 18:27
Hebrews 11:6
Hebrews 6:18 Philippians 4:12–13

Let Us Reason Together

God intends for us to live by faith in Him and to face all of life's difficulties by living close to Him and by doing what He says. This way He will accomplish through us what He planned since before the foundation of the world (Ephesians 1:4). He has given us everything we need for life and godliness through knowledge of *him* (2 Peter 1:3)!

Christ's life will be manifest through us as we live in close relationship with him, love Him with all our heart, mind, soul, and strength, and live a life of faith, trusting in Him in all things. There are so many promises to us in His Word, but He wants us to learn them for ourselves.

> But those who hope in the Lord
> will renew their strength.
> They will soar on wings like eagles;
> they will run and not grow weary,
> they will walk and not be faint.
>
> —Isaiah 40:31

He can make you soar above your circumstances.

The trials, difficulties and delays you are going through right now may make your God-given goals seem far in the distance, but God is your help. Hold onto His Word, and take hold of the following affirmation. Declare it into any situation in your life that currently looks impossible.

Affirmation

Nothing shall be impossible in my life!

WEEK 41

God's Divine Help

For the reader of this devotion this week, divine help is possible in your career journey—whether you are in a job looking for another job, you are an employer looking to transform your business performance, you are unemployed and looking for employment, or you are currently in the transition of switching careers.

It is so awesome to experience God's divine help. One day of His divine help is better than a lifetime of labor. His divine help delivers to you unsolicited help, people who don't know you will show up at the appointed time just to help you.

I recall God's divine help in my career journey. I had sent my resume to an organization for a job consideration. The human resources team called me in for an interview and shared with me that I will be meeting with three or four partners of the business. What happened next shocked me to continue to believe for God's divine help. A member of the team told me she was now revising my resume to meet the needs and expectation of these partners, and she will forward the revised copy to them, not my original resume. Now this is God's divine help.

Another receipt of divine help in the Bible was Moses. He received divine help from God to help lead the children of Israel out of bondage. That was no easy task, particularly with people who did not have confidence in Moses' ability to lead them. They grumbled, they conspired against him, undermined his leadership skills, and even caused Moses not to see the Promised Land. Nonetheless, God helped Moses by performing many miracles through him in the sight of Pharaoh, and demonstrated His wonders by creating a path for Moses through the Red Sea (Exodus 14:21–23).

My friends, this week, the Lord will volunteer help to you. He will intervene in your career situation even without being invited.

Philippians 2:13 Zechariah 4:6 Psalms 37:4
Exodus 14:21–23

Let Us Reason Together

What type of help do you need in your career situation this week? One of God's names is *Jehovah-Jireh*, "the Lord will provide." As Father, He provides all your needs. This thought alone can give you unwavering confidence.

Confess the following and receive it into your life. Your help will come from the Maker of heaven and earth.

Affirmation

I receive divine help!

WEEK 42

God Will Complete What He Started

As we near another year's end, find some time to reflect, not necessarily on what you have accomplished, but rather on what God has accomplished in you. Are you more at rest, calmer, more trusting, more relaxed, less anxious, less fearful, less stressed, less driven? Clearly from the beginning to the end of Scripture, we see how God is more interested in what is going on inside you than in your many accomplishments.

God is able to complete what He started in your life, if you will let Him. What He has promised He is able to perform (Romans 4:21). He is the author and the finisher of our faith (Hebrews 12:2). He is the beginning and the end of your life and mine. Look what He has promised.

> It is done. I am the Alpha and the Omega, the Beginning and the end. To the thirsty I will give water without cost from the spring of the water of

> life. Those who are victorious will inherit all this, and I will be his God and they will be my children.
> —Revelation 21:6

"For we are God's handiwork, created in Christ Jesus to do good works, which God prepared in advance for us to do" (Ephesians 2:10). Our work is to believe in, trust in, rely on Jesus, develop an intimate relationship with Him and find out what those works are and do them.

We all want to hear Jesus say these words to us at the end of our journey on earth, "Well done, good and faithful servant! You have been faithful with a few things; I will put you in charge of many things. Come and share your master's happiness!" (Matthew 25:21).

"As the deer pants for streams of water, so my soul pants for you, my God. My soul thirsts for God, for the living God. When can I go and meet with God?" (Psalm 42:1–2). God's first priority for you is that you desire Him as David did. Then He wants to make you a blessing.

"If anyone is poor among your fellow Israelites in any of the towns of the land the LORD your God is giving you, do not be hardhearted or tightfisted toward them," (Deuteronomy 15:7). He has chosen you to do the works of Jesus, and in order to do that, He must work in you to make you like Him.

Romans 4:21 Hebrews 12:2 Ephesians 2:10
Matthew 25:21
Psalm 42:1–2 Colossians 3:12 Deuteronomy 15:7

Let Us Reason Together

Every day is the day the Lord has made. Rejoice and be glad in it! (Psalm 118:24) Enjoy the beautiful creation God has given, the sea, the land, the birds of the air, the lilies of the field. Who you are on the inside will be reflected in whatever work you do. Bearing this in mind will help keep things in perspective and free God to bless you with the success He desires for you.

"Therefore as God's chosen people, holy and dearly loved, clothe yourselves with compassion, kindness, humility, gentleness and patience," Paul exhorted in Colossians 3:12. Declare and receive these qualities as you confess them into your life.

Affirmation

I am anointed with the spirit of compassion, kindness, humility, gentleness, and patience!

SECTION SEVEN

Being Light in a Dark World

WEEK 43

Soar Like an Eagle

What do you need to soar like an eagle? A while ago I was forwarded an email chain titled, "The 7 Principles of an Eagle." These principles resonated with me, and I believe it will for you too as you trust God to live out your best life during your career journey.

- **Principle 1**: Eagles fly alone at high altitude and not with sparrows or other small birds. Sometimes in your career journey, you have to learn to fly alone, not by popular opinion but by the leading of the Holy Spirit and your conviction.
- **Principle 2**: Eagles have strong vision. You need God to ignite your vision so you can remain focused no matter what the obstacle.
- **Principle 3**: Eagles do not eat dead things. They feed only on fresh prey. Steer clear of outdated and old information. Always do your research well.
- **Principle 4**: Eagles love the storm. When clouds gather, the eagles get excited. When we wait upon the Lord, we can use the storms of life to rise to greater heights. Achievers relish challenges and use them profitably.

- **Principle 5**: The eagle tests before it trusts. Whether in private life or in business, one should test the commitment of people intended for partnership.
- **Principle 6**: The eagle prepares for changes. Just as an eagle, we need to prepare for changes in family, career, ministry etc.
- **Principle 7**: The eagle knows when to retire. We occasionally need to shed off and retire old habits and vain items that ensnare us rather than adding value to our lives.[2]

Proverbs 27:17 Hosea 4:6 2 Timothy 2:15
Isaiah 40:31
1 Thessalonians 5:21 Ephesians 4:23 Ephesians 4:22

Let Us Reason Together

Do you want to soar like an eagle, strong, majestic in every area of your life? The promises of God found in Isaiah 40:31 are yours as you assert the following.

Affirmation

I am soaring like an eagle!

[2] Original principles taken from a sermon by Dr. Myles Munroe, "7 Principles of an Eagle," accessed at https://sharelife.wordpress.com/2007/08/22/7-principles-of-an-eagle-dr-myles-monroe/.

WEEK 44

Maintain Godly Priorities

The battle of a Christian job seeker, employer, or employee is very real, and there is always a temptation to be stressed. After all, you are a soldier from another dimension. It is often said that we are "in the world but not of the world." I am reminded of an expression I heard about work when I was a new Christian. When we went to work, we were going to "put on our earth suit." So whatever your position, you are really just a soldier in God's army—incognito, if you will.

Remember also the following principles about work as you seek employment or in your current position. We do not have to be anxious or stressed if we maintain our priorities in God's order.

- **Principle 1:** Do the best you can at whatever you are doing. We are here to do whatever we do or say to the best of our ability in Christ. We are living in eternity, and our work here is to make disciples of our Lord Jesus Christ. This does not always mean preaching. Doing the best job you can do may be the most important part of your work, whatever it is.
- **Principle 2:** A former pastor of mine (Carolyn) often referred to the Great Commission as the "family business." We are here to please Him, not be conformed to the world's

standards. He has instructed us not to "entangle ourselves with the affairs of this life," but to be always about our Father's business.

- **Principle 3:** God is supplying your needs as you continue to seek Him. We must always remember that our heavenly Father is our employer. Jesus instructed His disciples to choose to serve Him or money. If you have chosen to serve Christ, He has promised to take care of you. Just keep on seeking Him and letting Him work in your life.
- **Principle 4:** Your job is to live each day to the fullest. God is with you always, teaching you, training you, conforming you into the image of Christ. He loves you so much, He has chosen you to be a friend, a servant and a co-laborer with Him in spreading truth and love in this wicked world.
- **Principle 5:** All work is honorable, and God may be preparing you in your current position for a future assignment. But whatever He has you doing for the present, he expects you to be diligent, so He can provide your needs through the work He has given you. Learn to be a blessing in your current position even as you seek the Lord for His perfect plan for your life.
- **Principle 6:** You are where you are for a purpose. We are just passing through this life as ambassadors for Christ and carriers of His light. You are fulfilling your destiny in God no matter what it may look like or feel like for the moment.
- **Principle 7:** We are to live for His glory and not our own. Self-serving, ego-inflating ambition and self-exaltation are not godly objectives in the career life of a child of God.

1 Corinthians 10:31–33 2 Timothy 2:4
Matthew 6:24–33 Philippians 4:11–13
1 Thessalonians 4:11–12 Ephesians 6:14–20
1 Corinthians 1:26-31

Let Us Reason Together

Psalm 62:5 declares, "Yes, my soul, find rest in God; my hope comes from him." Fight distress with your faith, and declare the following affirmation.

Affirmation

I am relieved from my distress!

WEEK 45

Try Thanksgiving

The first reference to thanksgiving is, "thank" in the Old Testament, and occurs in 1 Chronicles 16:4 (NKJV) where David appointed some Levites to minister before the ark of the Lord, "to commemorate, to thank, and to praise the LORD God of Israel...with stringed instruments and harps...cymbals...trumpets."

The word for "thank" in this verse is, *yadah* (pronounced "*yaw-daw,*"' accent on the second syllable.) A study of this word reveals much, including the idea of an open hand. This would seem to indicate, in contrast with a closed hand, that we thank and praise our God because He is worthy of thanks and praise, but also, according to *Strong's Concordance,* the open hand indicates power. I believe that refers to the power and authority we have as God's children to receive blessings with an open hand from the One who owns it all.

A closed hand means we grasp and take ownership of God's gifts as something we own, when in reality everything belongs to God. You have surely noticed that when you praise and worship and give thanks to God you forget your troubles. When you get into the presence of the Lord, all worldly worries seem to melt away.

Worship and praise and thanksgiving are not intended only for the appointed Levites in the sanctuary of King David. This is for you and me everywhere and at all times. We call this *gratitude*, because God is worthy. His thoughts are higher than our thoughts, His ways higher than our ways.

> "For my thoughts are not your thoughts,
> neither are your ways my ways,"
> declares the LORD.
> For as the heavens are higher than the earth,
> so are my ways higher than your ways
> and My thoughts than your thoughts.
> —Isaiah 55:8-9

This passage, if you go ahead and read, talks about the wonderful generosity of God, His gifts to us that are all around—rain, snow, water, "seed to the sower, bread to the eater"—and the wonderful reminder that, "so is my word that goes out from my mouth: It will not return to me empty, but will accomplish the purpose for which I sent it" (v. 11).

Colossians 3:16–17 (NKJV) says, "Let the word of Christ dwell in you richly in all wisdom, teaching and admonishing one another in psalms and hymns and spiritual songs, singing with grace in your hearts to the Lord. And whatever you do in word or deed, do all in the name of the Lord Jesus, giving thanks to God the Father through him." So there is never a time when gratitude is not the appropriate response.

1 Chronicles 16:4 Isaiah 55:8–11 Colossians 3:16
Ephesians 5:20 1 Thessalonians 5:18 Philippians 4:6

Let Us Reason Together

Do you expend your energy complaining, or do you seek solutions through prayer, thanksgiving, and praise? Scripture encourages us to choose the second option. How self-involved are you? Assert the following into your life and experience the joy of gratitude:

Affirmation

I choose to have a grateful heart!

Snags or Opportunities to Serve?

> Keep this Book of the Law always on your lips; meditate on it day and night, so that you may be careful to do everything written in it. Then you will be prosperous and successful.
>
> —Joshua 1:8

Have you hit a snag in the road? Do you feel you have exhausted every option? Have you convinced yourself you have painted yourself into a corner? Have you made some choices you wish you could reverse? Do you feel you have missed God? Well, you can be sure the enemy of your soul will have done his job if you let these thoughts win the day.

The call of God on your life is never to compete with the world, learn its success formulas, or achieve burnout by overwork. The Lord has given you a new kind of life that bears little resemblance to the life you lived before. Success is not achieved through striving in the strength of the natural man.

"My grace is sufficient for you, for my power is made perfect in weakness," the Lord said to Paul (2 Corinthians 12:9).

Your strength is made perfect in weakness. Therefore, you must become less (decrease) while He must become greater (increase) (John 3:30). This way He lives His life through you. It is not a matter of you simply doing what you are naturally capable of doing. God wants to live His life through you. This is an amazing concept.

If you are in the workforce, you are on a mission field. Yes, you may be in preparation for something different down the road, but you are called to be where you are right now. You may be applying for jobs online. If so, that is your mission field. Your job is to perform that function as God gives you strength, and to have faith that God will provide.

Jesus came to serve; realize that you are here to serve also. Whether you are in management or at the bottom of the corporate ladder, whether you are a CEO or working in an entry-level position, you are there by the grace of God. Your job is to honor God and honor people in your work. No matter what trials you may experience, remember that you are co-laboring with Christ.

Meditate on the Word every day, and ask the Lord how to apply it to your life. Remember, He said if you would do so you would be prosperous and successful (Joshua 1:8). The Lord is guiding your path. Psalm 37:23 says that if the Lord delights is a man's way, He makes his steps firm.

2 Corinthians 12:9 John 3:30 Matthew 6:33
John 13:1–20
Joshua 1:8 1 Corinthians 3:9 Psalm 37:23

Let Us Reason Together

When the Lord calls, will you answer? Are you prepared to go wherever He leads and do whatever He says? Remember Samuel's words: "Speak, Lord, for your servant is listening" (1 Samuel 3:9).

Are you prepared to work at any place, at any time, and with anyone God chooses?

You are called to endure. During a time of crisis, you may feel that you are not able. That is when you are learning to rely on the strength of the Lord. Romans 15:4 encourages us that, "Everything that was written in the past was written to teach us, so that through endurance taught in the Scriptures and the encouragement they provide we might have hope." As you declare the following affirmation, receive the strength of the Lord.

Affirmation

I will endure!

WEEK 47

Let Your Light Shine

> But You are holy,
> O You who are enthroned in [the holy place where]
> the praises of Israel [are offered].
>
> —Psalms 22:3, AMP

This week, please journey with me through memory lane. As children we sang the old time gospel song, "This little light of mine, I am going to let it shine."

Is your light shining in your career situations? The Word of God in Matthew 5:16 proclaims, "In the same way, let your light shine before men, that they may see your good deeds and glorify your Father in heaven."

The tension and pressure of modern living draws wearily upon our energies, and sometimes they can snuff out our light. But in Christ we have the reassurance that, "In him we live, and move, and have our being" (Acts 17:28).

This text reminds us that God created us to shine. The secret is to maintain contact with God. This channels vitality and energy and constant replenishment into our being.

Friends, this week, I encourage you to let your light shine in your career situation—whether you are in a situation with a colleague, peer, or business partner, showing up for an interview, or simply meeting a client for a business meeting.

Remember you are light in darkness. You may be the only representative of Christ those you come in contact with will ever know. So go out this week and make Christ proud!

John 1:5 Matthew 5:16 Psalm 27:1 Psalms 22:3

Let Us Reason Together

The Bible declares that God inhabits the praises of His people (Psalm 22:3, KJV). How should we praise God? The Book of Psalms suggests giving Him glory by dancing, singing beautiful melodies, and playing musical instruments.

As you confess the following into your life in an attitude of praise and worship, so shall it be.

Affirmation

My light will shine!

WEEK 48

Operate From God's Perspective

> And whatever you do, whether in word or deed, do it all in the name of the Lord Jesus, giving thanks to God the Father through him.
>
> —Colossians 3:17

Work weeks have a beginning, a middle, and an end. We mark time in terms of weeks. We speak of "Monday through Friday," even though everyone's work week does not begin on Monday and end on Friday. We speak of the work week and the weekend—even if we work on the weekend. "Thank God it's Friday," we say (TGIF), so we get a couple of days off from work.

In the USA, Wednesday has typically been referred to as "hump day," the middle of the week—two days behind us, two days more until the weekend (when we don't work). Research has shown that large numbers of people hate their jobs. You don't even have to read the research. You know from what you have seen and heard. Maybe you yourself have hated your work. But God has a different perspective on work.

If you have chosen to serve God you will have a different perspective from the world on work and on prosperity. As many difficulties as you may experience as a Christian in and out of the workforce, God's Word and God's Spirit are always there to encourage you.

The Lord, speaking through Joshua, reminded the people of the many ways He had delivered them, and then said:

> But if serving the LORD seems undesirable to you, then choose for yourselves this day whom you will serve, whether the gods your ancestors served beyond the Euphrates, or the gods of the Amorites, in whose land you are living. But as for me and my household, we will serve the LORD.
>
> —Joshua 24:15

God always give us a choice. Every day is an opportunity to serve Him with gladness and gratitude. You may be called upon to choose to serve the Lord every day of your life, and you may have to trust Him as Abraham did, as He calls you "to the land I will show you" (Genesis 12:1).

Colossians 3:17 Joshua 24:1–15 Genesis 12:1

Let Us Reason Together

Prosperity is your heritage as a child of God. The Bible reminds us in Genesis 26:12–13 that "Isaac planted crops in that land and the same year reaped a hundredfold, because the LORD blessed him. The man became rich, and his wealth continued to grow until he became wealthy." Assert into your life the following, and so shall it be.

Affirmation

I will prosper!

WEEK 49

Be Sure You Are Bearing Fruit

The Bible talks about being fruitful. Matthew 3:10 says, "The axe is already at the root of the trees, and every tree that does not produce good fruit will be cut down and thrown into the fire."

What type of fruit are you producing as a business owner, at your place of employment, with your peers and colleagues and your boss?

Failure to bear fruit contradicts divine law or decree, and I pray for someone using the devotional this week that the Lord will cause you to experience all round fruitfulness, particularly in your career situation.

I recall a situation in my career situation when I was not bearing much fruit. I was unfulfilled in that situation. My recourse was to pray for a change of the situation, the grace to impact that situation for good and make it fruitful, or a different perspective for me to review the situation differently.

My friends, when we are in a situation that is fruitless, we must be willing to do a candid self-evaluation of the situation. This requires opening our mind to all possibilities, regardless of how painful the thought can be. Removing ourselves from the situation is not always the answer. I too have been tempted to run rather than face the situation boldly with the help of God through prayers. If you run, you may not have the opportunity to learn the lessons you are destined to learn that will propel you for maturity in your career journey.

Don't shortchange yourself from learning through life's experiences. Always remember the adage that says, "Experience is the best teacher."

Psalm 128:3 Genesis 49:22 Amos 9:14

Let Us Reason Together

This week as you go about your career journey, ponder with me this scripture in Genesis 17:6. "I will make you very fruitful; I will make nations of you, and kings will come from you."

As you reflect on this scripture, affirm the following into your life and so shall it be.

Affirmation

My life will be like a fruitful vine.

WEEK 50

Spread the Peace From God

This week we are going to be thinking about peace, about being still and quiet. These ideas seem to be anathema to the chaotic, frenzied world of work sometimes. And, unfortunately, our minds and spirits have become accustomed to this clamor of activity until we can have great difficulty hearing God. But deep inside we know God is calling us to a place of stillness and quiet. How do we attain that?

Being still and quiet may characterize your quiet time in the morning or at night, but when you are on the job you may be facing quite a different situation. However, the stillness and quiet that God offers is one that remains on the inside and carries you through the day. You may think of it as an anchor.

When you have made up your mind to seek the Lord with all your heart, soul, mind, and strength, you will be assailed from all sides with distractions, confusion, fear, doubt, temptation, and every other form of attack at the enemy's disposal. But the truth is that in knowing God, in becoming better acquainted with Him, you will develop the kind of peace that the enemy cannot disrupt. How awesome is that?

"Now acquaint yourself with Him, and be at peace," we read in Job 22:21 (NKJV). "Thereby good will come to you." Do yourself a favor and look this verse up in different versions. This one carries with it the sense of knowing God more personally, and this is the emphasis the Holy Spirit is after when He speaks of being still and knowing (Psalms 46:10) and in Psalms 131:2, below:

"But I have calmed and quieted myself, I am like a weaned child with its mother, like a weaned child I am content," David wrote. Whenever there is repetition, the objective is emphasis. "Like a weaned child...like a weaned child..." Think of what that means. "A weaned child with its mother" indicates that although the child is weaned from the mother's breast, he is still *with* the mother. The *New English Bible* even uses the words, "clinging to its mother." The *Amplified* includes, "ceased from fretting."

Other versions of Job 22:21, instead of "acquaint," say "submit to God" (NIV), or, "Come to terms with God" (NEB), but the King James uses "acquaint." In *Strong's Concordance,* we find the Hebrew *cakan',* "to be familiar with; by impl. To minister to, be serviceable to..." Pause and reflect on this!

Job 21:22 Psalms 46:10 Psalms 131:2
Hebrews 5:12–14 2 Timothy 2:20–21

Let Us Reason Together

In Job 13:15–16, Job says, "Though he slay me, yet will I hope in him; I will surely defend my ways to his face. Indeed, this will turn out for my deliverance, for no godless person would dare come before him!" No matter what your crisis situation is at this very moment, remember that you are His child and He is your Father. He is training you for great service. He is with you, He hears you and wants to use you.

You are growing in the Word, weaned from the milk, able to take the meat, but still clinging to God. You must learn to hear from Him, to be familiar with Him, and to *minister* to Him. He is making you *serviceable* for the kingdom of God, both now and in eternity. Begin to pronounce the following into your life, and so shall it be.

Affirmation

My soul is stilled and quiet.

WEEK 51

Find Favor With God and Man

Who can explain God's favor? Lord, You know everything about me. As the psalmist David says in Psalm 139:1–6:

> You know when I sit and when I rise;
> you perceive my thoughts from afar.
> You discern my going out and my lying down;
> you are familiar with all my ways.
> Before a word on my tongue
> you, LORD, know it completely
> You hem me in behind and before,
> And you lay your hand upon me.
> Such knowledge is too wonderful for me,
> too lofty for me to attain."

You know everything about me, yet I know that, because You are not a respecter of persons, You see me with favor in the same way You saw David with favor because he was a man after God's own heart, though he had sinned greatly. Although we have sinned and continue to battle with sin, You are merciful and grant favor, mercy, and compassion.

In Psalm 102:13, You say, "You will arise and have compassion on Zion, for it is time to show favor to her; the appointed time has come." God, your favor rests upon me in the most amazing way. I may never understand. Even before I believed, Your hand was upon me because You knew the end from the beginning. You knew that one day I would believe in You and in Your Son, Jesus Christ, and eventually give my life and all I am to You.

Psalm 139 Psalm 102:13

Let Us Reason Together

Whether you are seeking employment, facing a marital situation, struggling with a financial situation, or dealing with any other problem, what role is Christ playing in it?

Begin to claim the following affirmation for your life, and so shall it be.

Affirmation

I will find favor with God and man!

WEEK 52

Live a Life of Thanksgiving

Friends, God has been taking us through this career journey, and for that alone, we thank Him and give Him the highest praise.

Thanksgiving to God, especially for gifts and blessings received, is required and expected—even for those things not yet received.

God wants His children to thank Him and show gratitude for everything that happens. We are to continuously show appreciation for the many things we normally take for granted. Our willingness to thank God should not be situational.

Thanksgiving to God can be expressed in several different ways. However, offering thanksgiving to God in an acceptable manner guarantees an immediate response from God. The story of King Solomon comes to mind—he was so generous in his thanksgiving to God, and God responded to Solomon by giving him even the things he did not ask for. It is like receiving a blank check to write the amount you want on it.

Can you imagine God answering all your prayer requests and giving you even the things you have not thought of?

Resolve that no matter how difficult your career journey is, you will be thankful. Remember Thessalonians 5:16–17: "Rejoice always, pray continually, give thanks in all circumstances; for this is God's will for you in Christ Jesus."

I pray therefore that as you rejoice, praise God, and remain thankful for His goodness and mercy over your life, you will receive irreversible blessings from him in Jesus' name.

Psalm 92:1 2 Samuel 6:14 Psalm 138:1–3

Let Us Reason Together

Reflect again on the life of the psalmist David, and emulate his passion and desire to worship, praise, and thank the most high God. You will enjoy many benefits by doing this, but above all, you will be pleasing God. Have you praised God lately?

Accomplish this by declaring the following into your life and consistently acting on its principles.

Affirmation

I will rejoice and be thankful all the days of my life.

How to Find God's Will in Your Career

Ultimately, God is your source, not your career. The Bible says, "For in him we live and move and have our being" (Acts17:28).

To find God's will in your career, you must be willing to do the following:

Make Him Your Priority

Do not allow your career to usurp the place of God in your life. It is easy to fall into this trap because we live busy lives and can be consumed by situations at hand. However, we must remember who gave us life and the career of choice.

Shine for Jesus

In your career, shining for Jesus should be central to every decision you make. Test each decision by asking what Jesus would do in any given situation.

Be at Peace with Everyone You Deal with in Your Career Path

In this journey you will meet unkind and difficult people. However, the Bible instructs us in Hebrews 12:14 to "make every effort to live in peace with everyone and to be holy; without holiness no one will see the Lord." Strive for peace in all your relationships, both personal and work related.

Walk this Career Journey with Compassion

Luke 6:36 tells us to "be merciful [compassionate], just as your Father is merciful." Kindness and compassion are always appropriate, regardless of the person or place concerned. Treating others with respect and compassion goes a long ways towards promoting harmony in your career journey.

Be Wise

The Bible instructs us in Proverbs 24:14 that wisdom is sweet to our soul, and if we find it, there is a future hope for us. Our hope will not be cut off. Pray that God will give you wisdom in every decision you make and every step you take. Ask Him to show you His will and to give you the grace to honor Him in all your ways.

Spiritual Tips and Prayers for Your Career Journey

Tip 1: Cultivate an attitude of praise—even when you don't feel like it.

God inhabits the praises of His people, and your praise will move Him to action on your behalf.

> Enter his gates with thanksgiving
>   and his courts with praise;
>   give thanks to him and praise his name.
> For the LORD is good and his love endures forever;
>   his faithfulness continues through all generations.
>
> —Psalm 100:4–5

When you praise Him, God will crown your year with bounty and your carts will overflow with abundance.

Prayer Point

Holy Spirit, anoint and empower the reader of this devotional to praise You and worship You. To your glory, I pray this in Jesus' name. Amen.

Tip 2: Ask God for divine direction and guidance

You cannot navigate the journey of life on your own—even your own career; it is far too difficult and will lead to nothing but frustrations. But with God all things are made possible and easier (Mark 10:27).

> Show me your ways, LORD,
> teach me your paths.
> Guide me in your truth and teach me,
> for you are God my Savior,
> and my hope is in you all day long.
>
> —Psalm 25:4–5

Prayer point

Heavenly Father, give abundantly to the readers of this devotional divine direction and guidance in whatever situations they are in, and help them to make right decisions that will honor You and bless them. In Jesus' name, I pray. Amen.

Tip 3: Discover the power of belief

God is still in the business of working miracles. You just need to see it in your everyday life and believe that he is able.

> When he had finished speaking, he said to Simon, "Put out into deep water, and let down the nets for a catch." Simon answered, "Master, we've worked hard all night and haven't caught anything. But because you say so, I will let down the nets." When they had done so, they caught such a large number of fish that their nets began to break.
>
> —Luke 5:4–6

Prayer point

Most high God, strengthen the belief of the readers of this devotional and give them the ability to trust You, simply because You said so. Reward them with divine miracles that will surprise them. In Jesus' name, I pray. Amen.

Tip 4: Embrace passion

When you are passionate about a situation, you are driven to achieve results. Christ Himself had such great passion for our souls that He willingly laid down His life for us.

Nehemiah had great passion to rebuild the fallen walls of Jerusalem, and the Lord granted him favor before the king. God will also reward your enthusiasm and passion when you willingly embrace His plan for your life.

Prayer point

Great I Am, release Your anointing of passion upon the lives of the readers of this devotional to achieve great success in every area of their lives. In Jesus' name, may it be so. Amen.

Tip 5: Keep hope alive

Sometimes you may feel as though you cannot continue the journey. You may feel overwhelmed by your situation and lose all sign of hope. In these most desperate of times when your life seems unclear and your direction blurry, there is still hope if you will focus your attention on Jesus Christ.

> For in this hope we were saved. But hope that is seen is no hope at all. Who hopes for what he already has? But if we hope for what we do not yet have, we wait for it patiently.
>
> —Romans 8:24–25

Prayer point

Oh Lord, lift up the readers of this devotional and give them hope, even when there seems to be no hope. I pray this in Jesus' name. Amen.

Tip 6: Tap into the Power of Patience and Perseverance

Once you embark on your career journey, do not abandon it, for the results are decided at the end. You will need patience and the ability to persevere until the goal is achieved.

The scriptures use various images, such as running the race, to express the virtue of perseverance. This thought is reinforced in Galatians 6:9:

> Let us not become weary in doing good, for at the proper time we will reap a harvest if we do not give up."

Prayer point

Jehovah-Nissi, fill the readers of this devotional with the anointing of perseverance and patience. Help them to wait on You and to be assured that their change will surely come. In Jesus' name, I pray. Amen.

Tip 7: Exercise to relax and rejuvenate

Thomas Jefferson once said that a strong body makes the mind strong. You need to create a distraction from your career journey. Any form of exercise (at least thirty minutes a day) will provide relief from depression and anxiety, contribute to a positive self-image, and enhance feelings of optimism and enthusiasm.

Prayer point

Ancient of Days, renew and strengthen the readers of this devotional in body, soul, and spirit. In Jesus' name I pray this. Amen.

Conclusion

To enjoy the promises of God in your life and fulfill your destiny, you need salvation. If you are reading this devotional and have not accepted the Lord Jesus Christ into your life, we encourage you to give your life to the Lord by praying the following salvation prayer:

Lord Jesus, thank You for dying for me on the cross of Calvary and washing away all of my sins. To honor You, I dedicate myself to serving you all the days of my life in Jesus' name. Amen.

Remember, it is not His will that anyone of us should perish but have everlasting life. Without Christ, we are nothing and could never accomplish anything. If you allow Christ to journey with you in life—including your career—you will struggle less and trust more.

Now that you have taken a step of faith to trust our Lord Jesus Christ with your life, you can now view your career journey, as we earlier discussed in this devotional, as an opportunity for the Lord to do a new thing in your life. We offer for your spiritual consideration the following views to keep you focused:

- ➢ This journey is shaping and strengthening you for your greatness.
- ➢ God is refining you through this process.

- You are becoming a source of hope and inspiration to others if you go through this journey with grace.
- This journey allows you to recognize that God knows the end from the beginning.
- Through this journey, your soul is panting for God as the deer pants for streams of water.
- God is creating a spirit of humility in you and a dependence on Him. You cannot boast of yourselves or achievement because everyone can see that had it not been for the grace of God, you will not have overcome.

> You have also given me the shield of Your salvation;
> Your gentleness has made me great.
>
> —2 Samuel 22:36

About the Authors

Agnes Amos-Coleman

Agnes Amos-Coleman has been a business professional in the field of training, events, and marketing for more than twenty years. She holds an executive MBA from the University of Hull, United Kingdom.

She is also the Founder and CEO of Fellowship of Global Christian Job Seekers, a not-for-profit association dedicated to serving Christians all over the world who are unemployed or in transition, by sharing the message of hope and encouragement through uplifting news reports and motivational stories from around the world.

Dr. Carolyn Cogswell

Dr. Carolyn Cogswell has been involved in the ministry of praise and worship for more than thirty years and is a staff writer for Justin Peters, Songs For The Planet, Nashville, Tenn. She has a master's degree in family relations and child development with an emphasis in family studies from Oklahoma State University in Stillwater, and a Ph. D. in human ecology with an emphasis in child development from the University of Tennessee, Knoxville. She has worked as an educator and a journalist, and currently writes news, features, and music reviews for the *Topeka Metro Voice*, a publication celebrating faith, family, and community in northeast Kansas.

Made in the USA
Coppell, TX
28 March 2022